The 10 Laws
of
Lead-er-SHIP

So: Carol

Dr. Carolyn G. Anderson

C.H Anderson

You are a gift of life.
Keep Shining!

DEDICATION

This book is dedicated to you!

CONTENTS

ACKNOWLEDGMENTS

Thank You!

WHAT OTHERS ARE SAYING

"Dr. Carolyn G. Anderson defines "Leader" through her disciplined acts of intelligence, honesty, creativity, confidence, drive as well as courageousness. It is impossible for change not to occur when implementing all of these tools in this book. Through Dr. Carolyn's endless force, focus and commitment to see change, has given her the credibility to be a leader of leaders and the establishment of the Laws of Leadership. Her principles are superb!"

- **Alicia Perry – Counselor – Life Transformation Counseling Centers of America, Inc.**

"To be a leader you must first be a servant for at the end of the day leadership is a selfless act of service above self. Dr. Carolyn has been a humble servant leader who deeply cares for the well-being of those she leads. She speaks with the wisdom that comes from experience and has had her leadership style tried, tested and proven. This book will shift your life, business, career or relationships to the next level."

- **Dr. Daniel Thomas – MBBS Research Fellow – Caribbean Institute of Health Research (CAIHR)**

"Leadership guru Peter F. Drucker says leadership is 'lifting a person's vision to higher sights, raising their performance to a higher standard, and building their personality beyond its normal limitations.' That is Dr. Carolyn G. Anderson in a nutshell. She has done that for me, and for everyone she encounters. She is the embodiment of leadership!"

- **Reverend Darryl R. Williams – Senior Pastor – St. Stephen AME Church, Detroit, Michigan**

"Dr. Carolyn works relentlessly to equip, encourage and empower people to live their best life. She not only says it, but she models and lives it, which makes her a phenomenal leader. She leads by example."

- **Latreeta Burns – Social Worker – UnitedHealthcare of Wisconsin**

"Dr. Carolyn G. Anderson, is an astonishing, highly respected influencer and leading authority in her industry. Imbued with a gold mine of laser know-how and rare insights, Dr. Carolyn delivers simple, yet effective, life hack approaches that deposits a wealth of information and strategies, geared towards activating and releasing possibility within. She's impactful in significantly aiding you to breakthrough and move the pulse of your life upward into next levels unimaginable. Whether exposed to her directly or indirectly, just one dose of Dr. Carolyn's voice and high-beam brilliance will deeply impact your life – leaving you with enhanced, elevated, and positively enriched life."

- **Charisse Arrington – The Instant InSpirator - Life Becomes**

FOREWORD

When I began my career as an entrepreneur at 12 years old, selling Detroit Free Press subscriptions door-to-door back in 1983, I thought it was perfectly normal and natural for all kids to earn $100-$200 working 2-3 hours per night. As this continued I was able to save lots of money to buy my racing road bicycle, a boom box, a new pair of Nike's, and pretty much whatever else I wanted because I had earned it through my own efforts.

As I became a young adult, I realized I was different and wondered why was I able to do this those in my age group were not able to earn anywhere near this amount? Some of them were given money by their parents, but most went without, which led to them having little to no confidence as they grew older.

What I discovered was that those who take the self-**leadership** role in their lives at an early age develop confidence to eventually lead themselves and others on bigger stages. I discovered that the world was full of two kinds of people: leaders (the tiny minority) and followers (the vast majority) and Dr. Carolyn definitely falls within the tiny minority that was a leader since the age of 10. Which kind of person do you believe you are?

I learned that successful people have made decisions early in their lives to live their life on their own terms by taking the leadership role in their lives and pursing their dreams, goals and visions. Guess what, if you've not made these early decisions, good news, you're not too late. You can immediately apply the principles in *"The 10 Laws of Leadership"* and become a part of the "tiny minority."

I have learned and live by the mantra that leadership is not 'given' to you but needs to be 'taken' by you! Those who don't wait for others approval and take the leadership role in their lives ultimately are in the best position to create their own destinies!

In this powerful book written by **Dr. Carolyn G. Anderson**, you will learn how to understand your purpose, define your values and beliefs and come to understand that 'you' are the leader that our earth so desperately needs at this time. You will also learn that leaders are both born and made. If you were not born a leader, you will learn how to become one and contribute to the greater good of earth.

In *The 10 Laws of Leadership*, Dr. Carolyn will provide you with self-assessment tools to build your character and lead with integrity. Furthermore, she will assist you in understanding the differences between how she leads vs. how (he) leads and how these styles impact relationships both at home and in the business world. You will learn how to strengthen your own leadership skills by applying her ten laws to any area of your life. Get ready!

When you follow the formulas and strategies in this book, you will discover that you are the captain of your ship, the creator of your destiny, and the mentor and coach to others as the leader that they desire you to be to help them overcome their challenges, obstacles, and adversities. When you apply these ten laws to your life you will become an unstoppable force of power fully capable of achieving all your dreams, goals and aspirations.

The 10 Laws of Leadership teaches how to acquire specific knowledge and skills needed to lead yourself, your family, your business and your community. In doing so you will achieve all that you have ever desired in life and will become an inspiration for others to learn from you and do the same in their lives. You will learn that the role of leaders is not to capture more followers but to birth more leaders.

Throughout this book you will learn that you are the driving force to become the change the world needs to see in order to create a better life for you, your legacy and those that will come after you. Allow Dr. Carolyn to be the captain that guides your life to become an even better leader of today. This book is about transformation and grasping the fundamental principles of leadership.

Get ready for an amazing sail! Have your passport ready, book your trip, know who's coming with you, get on board, do the safety checks, become familiar with your cabin, meet the crew, and get your happy face on. You are about to embark on a life's journey with **Dr. Carolyn** as she teaches you how to transform lives, families, communities and businesses, one life, one family, one community, one business at a time. The journey starts now!

Enjoy!

Patrick Snow

PREFACE

Who am I? What's my Purpose? What on earth am I here for? Am I a leader? Was I born to lead? Were leaders born or made? Who are the leaders today? What does true leadership look like today? These have been some of the questions that have echoed over the years in one's pursuit to understand existence, purpose and leadership. These questions exist regardless of race, color, ethnicity, economic class, religious status or gender. Today, these set of questions are still being asked especially as it relates to leadership, entrepreneurship and influencers who are making global, international, local and daily life decisions that have significant impact on one's daily life.

"Leadership is not a title, it's a behavior."

Dr. Patricia Greco

On the 18th of July in the year 1918 in the village of Mvezo in Umtata, a leader was born. This leader was given the forename to Rolihlahla, meaning "troublemaker." It would seem that this leader's name predicted a doomed future at an early age. However, a troublemaker or not, this young leader knew that he was destined for more than what his name meant. Therefore, he started his quest to discover his life's purpose, to see what he was born and created to be and to do.

Rolihlahla's early days had its share of troubles and trials. He was arrested several times as a youth, not for stealing, bullying or any such acts of crime, but for standing for justice for his people. He was very vocal and had a strong belief system at a very early age. He was known amongst his peers as one they could look up to for assistance and guidance even when he was sentenced to prison.

As the years went along, Rolihlahla would rise from being a **PRISONER** for 27 years to a **PRESIDENT**. He led a very divided and segregated nation to unity. This leader who was once known as a troublemaker, and he did get in trouble, the first to attend school in his family, studied law, and renamed by his teacher Miss Mdingane, was the one and only, **Nelson Mandela**. He was the epiphany of leadership. He is one of the world's greatest leaders known to mankind. He demanded respect, simply by his presence. One could say, he was born a leader.

A very divided South Africa, highly political and lots of war, the country continued to face many trials and tribulations. There was turmoil amongst the people. Nevertheless, regardless of how bad things are and no matter what the circumstances may be, when a Leader uses his or her behavior to demonstrate leadership, it speaks volumes without ever opening his or her mouth. Such was the case with President Nelson Mandela. He didn't just articulated leadership, he showed it through his behavior.

Not only was South Africa divided amongst its people, so was its sports. One of the more popular sport in South Africa is Rugby. It's a sport similar to American Football, mixed with some Soccer and is said to be originated in England during the early 19th century. In its simplest form, the game is played by running with the ball in hand using an oval-shaped ball on a rectangular field with a H-shaped goalpost. The team consists of 15 players and the main reason why it's considered divided and so hated by Blacks, is because out of those 15 players, none, perhaps maybe one or two players were blacks. It is mostly an all-white team and South Africans who were blacks did not get to be a part of the team. Consequently, they also did not attend the games, and this led to blacks revolting and protesting against the sport of Rugby.

Until one day an act of leadership changed the trajectory of South Africa, the world and what true leadership is about. Something happens when true leaders demonstrate leadership through his or her actions and not just having a title and do nothing. President Nelson Mandela decided that the fight for unity has been along and even though there were progress, something drastic needed to be done in order to unite the nation. On June 24, 1995, Mandela and South Africa were triumphant. He saved a country by pulling on that green and gold jersey with a prancing antelope on the left breast. The Springboks were dear to the hearts of South Africa's white Afrikaners and loathed by the nation's black majority. By donning their emblem, Mandela reconciled a nation fractured and badly damaged by racism and hatred.

The South African captain, Francois Pienaar, was stunned that President Nelson Mandela showed up at the game. "Not in my wildest dreams did I think that Nelson Mandela would pitch up at the final wearing a Springbok on his heart," he said in a television interview some time later. He went on to say that when the President walked into their changing room to say good luck to them and when Mr. Mandela turned around, Pienaar noticed that he was wearing his number on the back of his jersey. It was an amazing feeling, noted Pienaar.

One day at a Rugby game, Mandela decided to attend. His attendance was not merely to be amongst the spectators, but to be a change agent. He wore the jersey color of the Rugby South African Team, amidst his supporters saying he should. He walked on the field and congratulated the captain of the team. That action was the beginning of a united country. His actions demonstrated that leadership is more than a title, it's a behavior. Leadership is about influence, it's about loyalty, love, purpose, drive, tenacity, whit, vulnerability and taking a stand. It's about seeing a problem and being the solution. All it takes is one person to have a determination and a drive to see change. This one person can be you. Source: http://www.nydailynews.com/sports/more-sports/mandela-sports-unite-racially-divided-south-africa-article-1.1539151

Purpose of the Book

Thus, the purpose of the book is to revisit and re-build the framework for authentic leadership, so that aspiring, emerging and/or established leaders can arise and step into his or her place of influence and authority and be the change that earth longs for. Within these pages are questions, applications, to-do's, and stories of different leaders, their leadership styles, some leaders that failed, and how they rose above their circumstances and became successful. What did they do differently that made them succeed? Allow this book to be a guide that you can use to re-establish leadership and to re-build the pillars of what true leadership is all about.

Throughout the pages of this book are numerous examples and principles that can be used as a blueprint for learning and understanding the core of Leadership. Leadership is such a widely used word with so many definitions, and, so one of the purposes of this book is to help to define leadership in its simplest form. It doesn't have to be complicated. Leadership is about leading authentically, living purposefully, amidst chaos.

With all the noise and social media craze and all that's happening in and around the world, how can one remain steadfast, focused and lead well at the same time? It is possible, and this book offers insights to remaining sane while leading and living life fully every day intentionally. I also shed some light on where I believe Leadership took the wrong turn and how to get back on track. Allow the stories, examples, principles and action items to take you on a journey like never before as we embark on a new voyage together. Are you ready?

 NOTES..........

In your own words, what is your understanding of the Purpose of the Book?

So, What? Why should anyone care?

Why should anyone care about re-building the pillars and fundamentals of Leadership? What's the **<u>significance</u>** of having a book that reshapes, rebuilds and reestablishes leadership at its best? After all, all is well, right? Don't fix it if it's not broken, because, those in leadership roles today are doing what's best for those they lead, right? Leaders should be able to live their lives the way they want to without any accountability to their followers, right? Everyone should be able to do what they want, with no care in the world and live in a chaotic environment with no order, correct? Well, hopefully you're **<u>SCREAMING NO</u>** at the top of your lungs.

Every day Leaders and/or Influencers in various sect of life, whether in business, the church, school, home, government, media and so forth are responsible for making decisions that can change the trajectory of one's destiny. Thus, it's exceptionally significant that there are some fundamental principles that leaders should exuberate considering that some of the decisions being made are life and death. Decision's such as, do the country go to war or not? Should we warn the people that there's a possibility that the water is polluted? Should we raise the interest rate? Should we foreclose on that house? Decisions about what is taught in schools. Decisions about healthcare and preventative medicine. Decisions about flight routes and safety issues. Decisions that affects the environment, religion, media, family, businesses, finance, marriages, atmosphere, banking, travel, and just about every single area of life.

Decisions are being made daily, whether good or bad that affects our tomorrow and the days to come. We all make decisions daily. We decide to get up or stay in bed, to work or not, what to eat, which way to drive, how much to spend, etc. However, these decisions are somewhat personal. The decisions become critical when they are being made that can affect the population at large. Therefore, it is imperative that leaders are leading with moral **character** and making decisions that are right and that's why this book is exceptionally **significant**. One could say it's the **blueprint** for re-establishing leadership and laying the foundation for what true leadership is all about.

 **NOTES..........**

In your own words, why is this book significant?

INTRODUCTION

"A Leader is one who knows the way, goes the way and shows the way."

John C. Maxwell

Once upon a time, when the word Leadership was mentioned, most often it was associated with authoritative figures, such as Gandhi, Mandela, Lady Teresa, Presidents of various countries and other household names from different spheres of influence such as Oprah Winfrey, Michael Jordan and so forth. These figures were considered to be leaders as they embodied certain characteristics that demonstrated to their followers that they were worthy to be listened to. They didn't need to announce to their followership or anyone for that matter that they were leaders or used their title to validate their leadership. This was because, as John Maxwell mentioned above, they led by example. They knew who they were, where they were going, and they showed how they got there and how their followers could get there also. They made leadership look easy, even though it wasn't and still isn't.

Leaders then, were highly respected individuals, revered, admired and some even idolized. A notable characteristic of Leadership was that the role demanded respect. Whether the leader was deemed to be a good leader or bad, their followers respected them, because if they didn't they wouldn't follow him or her. Other noticeable characteristics were the **moral and ethical** standards of the Leader. Most of the leaders demonstrated their moral and ethical values, and their genuine love and care for the people, based on the decisions that they were making. Leadership then was pure, and it wasn't so much about the leaders themselves as it was about doing what was right, fair, honest and just, even if it meant denying themselves a peace of mind for the common good, such as Gandhi and Dr. Martin Luther King, Jr.

It was very rear to have leaders that were intentionally immoral or sought to destroy the people they led, except for a few leaders such as Adolf Hitler and other dictators. They were not the norm, but rather the exception and were not ones that most people grew up saying that they wanted to be like. Most Leaders meant well, led well, were revered, respected and were recognized for their Leadership to the point of earning Nobel Peace Prize Awards.

Leadership today, seems to be a very loosely used word and almost at times a joke. It seems that society have lost the respect for what true leadership is and surely, they cannot be blamed considering that so many leaders have fallen or have caused the followers to lose respect and trust in them. The office of the United States Presidency is not even a position that is revered anymore or seen by society as the epiphany of leadership as it was historically, and that's unfortunate. Whether the people liked the reigning President or not, the office itself was respected.

Recently, I was in a Pageant and one of the questions that was asked of me, was my opinion on a decision that the President of the United States had made. In my response, I started off by saying that, because I am a United States Army Veteran, we view what the presidents say differently. The President is the **Commander in Chief** of the Military and when they speak, it's an order, and our opinions are neither here nor there. While internally a soldier or veteran may not agree with the choices and decisions that's being made, the office of the president still has to be respected in our eyes.

 "Getting the SHIP back to shore"

Dr. Carolyn

Unfortunately, today, some of these offices are outright disrespected and disregarded and I can see why. Society as a whole seemed to have lost hope and trust in the essence of leadership, and they really can't be blamed because the character of some of the leaders are tainted. The behavior of a leader is best shown through his or her character and not just the title he or she holds. **Character** as defined by Merriam Webster1 is "one of the attributes that makes up and distinguishes an individual." Take for example, if the leader's character is deemed to be more humanitarian and/or a people person, what you will tend to find is that the people that will follow that leader share some of the same traits, beliefs and characteristics. The character of presidents, prime ministers, kings and queens, pastors, governors, CEO's and those that are gatekeepers over nations, should demand respect without saying, but most of them are not. What happened? What changed? Something shifted!

The **SHIP** went off course and started drifting away in an open sea and can't seem to find its way back on course. The SHIP is way off on no-man's island and the navigational system is not working. There's no communication between the lost, the hopeless and because so much time have past, no one is looking for the **SHIP** anymore. Well, the time has arrived to get **Lead-er-SHIP** back on course and re-establish the new direction with an upgraded navigational system. It's time to create an efficient and effective guide to be used to map out the fundamental steps that are necessary for the journey and to find the lost and hopeless. The time has come for a generation of **Generals** and **Captains** that are ready to Lead and get things back on the right path. Leaders don't have to know all the

---

1 MerriamWebster.com

answers before getting started, but what they do need is guts, stamina, loyalty, love, whit, drive, patience, integrity and perseverance, and character, just to name a few, to get going.

It is impossible to attempt to understand what leadership is all about, without knowing one's purpose. It is a mistake that leaders often make by taking on a leadership role without knowing his or her authentic purpose and reason for existence. It is the **First Law of Leadership - PURPOSE**: Thus, the time is now for emerging, current and even seasoned leaders to validate or re-establish his or her true purpose. I believe that many are ready for a change. I hear the cries through various communication channels that people are ready to be led and to lead authentically. So, I ask, are you ready to put into action "**The 10 Laws of Leadership**?" You could be the Leader of today that earth is waiting for. Are you ready?

Do you believe you are a Leader? Why or why not?

What are the leadership traits or characteristics that you believe that you have? Explain

Do you believe that leaders are born or can be made? Explain

What have you learned so far?

What can you apply now?

NOTES..........

CHAPTER 1

LAW #1: WHO AM I? WHAT'S MY PURPOSE?

> *"The greatest tragedy in life is not death, but life without a reason."*
>
> **Dr. Myles Munroe**

In the last section, I shared how the character of the Leader is important as it shapes how he or she leads. I shared that one of the common mistakes that leaders make is to get into a leadership positions without understanding his or her purpose. When a leader leads without knowing his or her purpose, it's like leading blindly with no sense of direction and he or she will end up somewhere, but not where he or she needs to be. It's not the right place.

Authentic Leadership is when one knows without the shadow of a doubt what he or she was created to be and to do. It's critical that leaders understand and know his or her reason for existence. It is only when a leader understands what he or she was born to be and to do, can that leader lead effectively.

"Your Purpose Matters"

Dr. Carolyn

Tweet

The questions of existence or purpose are not new phenomenon's or new quests. In fact, "Philosophers such as Plato, Aristotle, Socrates and others throughout the ages have attempted to explore these seemingly illusive questions. For the most part, their efforts have ended in more questions than answers." These questions continue to be asked from generation to generation, from leaders and followers, from college graduates, life coaches, entrepreneurs, authors, designers, executives, researches, speakers, to army veterans and so on.

It is extremely important to understand your own existence as it brings a sense of fulfilment and contentment. It is not a good thing to simply be alive and not living life with meaning or without knowing your purpose in life. It is an unfortunate truth that many people live with a quiet desperation and some die plagued by the vague uneasiness that somehow, they have "missed it." Others wander aimlessly and a few live purposefully attempting to solve

2

the puzzle posed by life (Munroe, 1992, p. 57). When an individual knows his or her purpose or even when one knows the purpose of a thing, it creates meaning and value.

The same is true for leaders, when they know their reason for existence, it makes it easier to lead and serve. Without knowing why one exists it leads to confusion and sometimes frustration as life is more than "a quest for pleasure, as Freud believed, or a quest for power, as Alfred Adler taught, but rather a quest for meaning" (Frankl, 2006, p.10). When life is lived with meaning and purpose, it makes life happier, more fruitful and rewarding. It creates excitement and anticipation for what each day brings.

"The first step on the journey to finding purpose is to write the vision"

Tweet

Dr. Carolyn

One of life's greatest tasks is that he or she would find meaning in life (Frankl, 2006), and when that meaning is established, it becomes a ripple effect, which transcends into a more fruitful life, healthier family structure, healthy communities, transformed cities and eventually a better world. When there's meaning, one doesn't have to worry about what life may bring. So, where do we start?

Write the Vision

"The poorest person in the world is not the one that has no money but it's the one that has no vision."

Dr. Myles Munroe

Every new journey in life begins with taking the first step. Whether it's a baby learning how to start walking, a man or woman desiring to start a business, an individual who desires to become a pilot, walk on the moon, or one who desires to know his or her true authentic purpose, it all starts with taking that first step. Once you've taken that first step, the 2nd, 3rd, 4th and remaining steps become much easier to accomplish.

Great leaders are continually growing and exploring their understanding of themselves. Self-awareness and personal vision statements are key in helping the leader to live a more purposeful life. These principles not only improve their leadership styles but also the lives of those they influence. Leaders should not attempt to get others to change without changing themselves first. When Leaders focus on self-development then it becomes second nature for those in their midst to follow suit.

There are many who have no vision for their lives and wonder how to obtain one. There are others who have a vision but are stuck in the mud of confusion not knowing what to do next. Then there are those who had a vision but have abandoned it because of discouragement, disillusionment, some measure of failure, opinions of others, derailment or frustration.

Tweet

"A Vision is something you see with your mind and not with your physical eyes"

Dr. Carolyn

A Vision is something you see with your mind. It's not something tangible that you can touch. It's the BIG picture of where you see yourself, now, and in the future. It's being able to visualize your BIG dream, your BIG life, your destiny. When one has a Vision, it makes decisions easier to make, because he or she makes the choices based on whether or not it aligns with his or her Vision. Having a Vision is like a navigation system, where you are able to enter the desired destination before actually getting there.

When I started Integrity Consulting and Coaching Firm (www.carolynganderson.com), it all started with writing the Vision, not just for myself, but for our Client's and Coachee's as well. It's the foundation of the business and it's what has gotten the Firm to where it is today. This book is a part of that BIG Vision. I knew that I would write many books and that one of them would be about leadership, I just didn't know exactly when. I had the title and contents of the book written down, way before I started writing the book. This is what having a Vision does. You are able to see things with your mind, before seeing it with your physical eyes.

It was a vision that produced ink, pen, paper, computers, television, buttons, houses, telephones, eyeglasses, contact lenses, water bottles, trains, planes, garage door openers and pretty much any and everything you can think of. Vision is where every idea and invention started. However, having a VISION in the mind and keeping it there is one thing; but having it and writing it brings one closer to fulfillment. No product or service would exist today, if the Vision was not written down. Therefore, to be an effective leader, the **VISION** must be written down, clearly, so that you can take what you have being seeing in your mind, to now seeing it on paper. In order for purpose to be in motion, the Vision in the mind has to be written down. It's the image that you need to see that will remind you where you're going.

"Your feet will never take you, where your mind has never been."

Author Unknown

Seeing the written Vision, helps to put one back on track, should he or she becomes overwhelmed or side tracked. This does happen quite a bit. Writing this book was quite a task. So many times, I could have given up, because (life happens), right?

However, when I glance upon my written Vision Statement, I am reminded that it's not about me or my frustrations, but it's about re-building the pillars of leadership. It's about a nation, a city, a community, an industry, a business, an organization, a family, a marriage, that's awaiting to lead and live purposefully and intentionally. It's about **you** that's reading this book. It was written with you in mind, knowing that the contents within these pages would be a tool that you can use in your toolbox to transform your life, your career, city, nation, business and/or organization. It's about leading authentically, living purposefully, amidst a chaotic world.

Tweet

"Lead Authentically, Live Purposefully, Amidst Chaos"

Dr. Carolyn

Having a written **Vision** declares, announces, reminds and proclaims where you are going and let people know more about who you are. If every **organization** has a vision, (at least they all should), then you should have one for your life, your family and your business, if you have a business. When one doesn't have a Vision, it's like dying a slow death with no hope. Without Vision he or she is perishing every day. The inability to see the light at the end of the tunnel is the same as having no Vision. Everything seems dark and even though the sun rises daily, it's of no significance because a lack of Vision creates darkness.

According to Dr. Myles Munroe, having a Vision is the source and hope of life. He further went on to say that one of the greatest gift ever given to mankind is not the gift of sight, but the gift of vision. Why? Sight is a function of the eyes; and vision is a function of the mind. You can't see your Vision with your physical eyes, but rather with your spiritual eyes, which is a part of your mind. While the brain houses the mind, it's not something that you can see with the physical eyes. Eyes that look are considered common, but according to Munroe (2003), eyes that see are rare." Therefore, having a Vision is so imperative as it's the first step towards understanding purpose and writing the Vision makes things clear.

Without vision and purpose, leadership is null and void. Attempting to lead without knowing where one is going is a dangerous task. All great exploits and expeditions worthy of mentioning or even those unknown that were and are successful, started with a Vision. Vision is a source to be reckoned with. It precedes the inventions of airplanes, the vessels of ships, the batteries in cars, the cement in the building, the telephone that rings, the bag that is carried and the book that is read.

"Vision sees before the eyes do"

Dr. Carolyn

Tweet

8

Once all blurriness is removed from one's Vision and he or she is able to articulate it, then the next step is to get that Vision on paper. Doing so creates a Vision Statement. When the Vision is seen with the mind and can be conceptualized in writing, it's then that the statement is clear and the Vision kicks into motion.

Vision Statements

Without having and writing a Vision it's like building a house with no blueprint and having no idea of how the end product will be. It's building blindly, trusting that the Contractor will build what you desire. Many live their lives this way, having others dictate their days, their years and their life. They just work tirelessly every day, being overworked and overwhelmed and being really busy, but end up accomplishing nothing. In the end, they have nothing to show for their lives and so many years have passed by and they are not sure how they ended up where they are today. This is why it's necessary to write your own Vision and to make it very plain so that you don't perish.

Writing a Vision Statement is a simple task for me but can be very daunting for many. I have been teaching and coaching hundreds, on writing their Vision Statements, Mission Statements, and Purpose Statements. In its simplest form, I want to get you started on writing your Vision Statement. **The 10 Laws of Leadership** book, is not like other books that's just for reading purposes or intellectual knowledge. It is a hands-on, practical, how-to book that you can use over and over again. It can be used in Churches, Colleges, Corporations, at Conferences, Home Schoolers, Organizational Trainings, Leadership Institutes, Communities and anywhere and for anyone that desires to live life with meaning and purpose. It for anyone who desires to lead his or her life and to be an example to and for others.

A Vision Statement is very precise and should not be more than one to two sentences. It can take a while to come up with a Vision Statement that tells the story of who you are and what you do in one sentence, one phrase or one cliché, but it's doable. Chad's Vision Statement below, took him awhile to narrow down while I coached him through it. Most adults tend to be very wordy and want to tell an entire chapter about who they are, and so it can be very difficult to write a precise Vision Statement. Below are examples of Vision Statements:

"Transforming lives one life at a time"
Carolyn G. Anderson

"World class change agent becoming better daily"
Chad Uebele

"To Live a Legacy and Leave a Legacy"
K. Anthony Anderson

It is important to have a Vision statement because it:

1. Gives you ongoing motivation and inspiration to work on your purpose

2. Influences all decision-making and choices

To get you started, answer the questions below:

1. What legacy or footprint do you want to leave behind?

_____

_____

_____

_____

_____

_____

_____

_____

_____

_____

_____

_____

_____

_____

2. If you were a reporter writing about your success what would you be saying?

3. Jot down some words that describes you.

4. What would you do with your life if you knew without the shadow of a doubt that you could not fail, and that money was not an issue and you had no fears?

5. What is your high-level, big dream for your life? What do you see yourself doing happily every day?

6. Combine your answers (1+2) in the previous questions into one sentence.

Let's start putting it together…

Based on your answers above, begin to jot down some sentences and phrases that you believe is a good Vision statement that describes you.

Hopefully by now you are starting to feel like you're going somewhere. I am excited for you! You may not have it all together and your Vision Statement may not be exactly what you want it to be. However, if you have written anything down so far, you are much further than most adults. Every great accomplishment starts with the first step. By writing or even envisioning your Vision, you are taking that first step and I congratulate you. Be proud of your leadership journey.

Sometimes people *be-little* themselves and allow *what I call "little me"* to have a say so about who they are. It's that little negative, annoying voice that some people have. It whispers comments such as ***"you're not good enough, you're not going to make it, or you're not qualified to lead, etc.,"*** It's very condescending and highlights what's not good or going well. That's not the voice that you want to listen to. It's time to **THINK BIG** and shut down (the *little voice*) …Get excited and be encouraged about where you would like to see your life today, tomorrow and in the future.

Write the Vision and make it plain

Keep Writing...

It's time to start narrowing down what you have written so far. Don't overanalyze your Vision statement, just write some of the first thoughts that comes to mind. Remember it doesn't need to be a long sentence. It can be a phrase, cliché, or a statement.

As a refresher, my BIG PICTURE VISION STATEMENT is: **"Transforming Lives, one life at a time" Carolyn G. Anderson**

Write your Vision Statement

Congratulations on what you have written thus far. You can always come back and revise it. In addition, there's a Vision & Mission Course and Purposefinder™ Coaching online at (www.carolynganderson.com), that are excellent sources that you can use with this book.

Once you have written your **BIG PICTURE VISION STATEMENT**, rehearse it over and over again and say it out loud without having to reference back to the written version. Share it with friends, family, co-workers, colleagues, and those you come in contact with. Speak it out loud, so that you can hear the sound of your Vision. Announce it to the world on your social media platforms or network and let people know where you are going and your new direction. Let it sink in, because you are one step closer towards knowing and understanding the authentic you. Your leadership journey has begun. CONGRATULATIONS!!

Write down your BIG Vision Statement again?

Don't worry as you go through this book, you will get a chance to come back and alter it, should you feel the need to.

ACTION STEPS!

TO DO!

Write your **BIG VISION** down for 21 days! According to Dr. Caroline Leaf it takes at least 21 days for a new habit or behavior pattern to start in your mind. Therefore, to truly get your new Vision to sink in, write it down for 21 days as you continue to go through the pages of this book.

BIG Vision Statement:

1. _____

_____

2. _____

_____

3. _____

_____

4. _____

_____

5. _____

_____

6.

7.

8.

9.

10.

11.

12.

13.

14.

15.

16.

17.

18.

19.

20.

21.

NOTES..........

What is your understanding of having a Vision or Vision Statement?

Maximizing your Mission

"The measure of who we are is what we do with what we have."

Vince Lombardi

Now that you have established or at least got started on writing your **Vision Statement**, the next step in working towards establishing your purpose and becoming that excellent leader that you are, is to write your **Mission Statement**. A mission statement is directly tied to your Vision Statement as it clearly states the steps that you will take to fulfill your Vision.

I have seen several organizations that have their **Mission and Vision Statements backwards**. From major corporations to small businesses and key influencers, their Mission Statement is really their Vision Statement and vice versa. The word mission, is a derivative of the word Missionary. A true Missionary is always on a mission, traveling, doing their work. For example, Mother Teresa, when she was alive, she was constantly on the go. Every time she was shown on television, she was on some form or a mission's trip. Her life's purpose was on the mission field, per se. When she completed one mission, or helped one family, she continued the journey to accomplish all that she was set out to do.

Thus, a mission statement or having a Mission, are action steps. It is the steps that will be taken to carry-out the Vision that's in place.

If you recall, your **Vision Statement** is the **BIG** Picture. You can visualize your Vision and it should look really good, but how are you going to accomplish that **BIG VISION**? Well, that's what a Mission Statement is. Your mission statement is the written plan of action (the directions), the roadmap that one takes to get to the destination. When writing a Mission Statement, it can be very wordy. Your Mission statement can be more than one sentence and can be bulleted. You mission statement is not something that you need to remember, like you do your Vision, because the Mission is what you do, not what you see.

As a refresher, my **Vision Statement** is **"Transforming Lives one Life at a time"** and the **Mission Statement** that is used to carry out that Vision is:

"Lives will be transformed through my coaching, mentoring, ministering, writing, sharing information, hosting events, speaking, media outlets, all while maintaining balance and being authentic" **Carolyn G. Anderson**

As you see, it can be wordy with complete sentences, phrases, or bullet points. It's simply writing out completely the necessary steps that you believe will be needed to carry out the Vision. There's really no limit or limitations to the context or content that makes up the Mission Statement.

For simplicity purposes, write down your Vision Statement that you have crafted. This will make it easier to formulate your Mission Statement, rather than flipping back to those pages.

Write down your BIG Vision Statement again?

Write down your Mission Statement? What steps will you need to fulfill your Vision?

Write your Mission Statement

Congratulations you have written your Mission Statement!

What are your takeaways?

What did you learn so far?

What are you going to apply now?

NOTES..........

Journal the Journey – Notes from this Chapter

NOTES..........

Journal the Journey – Notes from this Chapter

CHAPTER 2

LAW #2: VALUES AND BELIEFS

"When your VALUES are clear to you, making decisions becomes easier."

Roy E. Disney

Your purpose, drive and leadership are heading in the right direction. You have just completed **Law #1** on the journey of understanding the **10 Laws of Leadership**. You should have established your Vision and Mission Statements and learned more about yourself. I asked you a few questions that were meant to probe you to go deeper in your thoughts and get you to look within yourself for answers. They are within you and one of my goals is to help you to see that. This book is a probe and a workbook to help you become the great leader that you are. You are on your way towards understanding your Purpose, Leadership Style and to learn tools and techniques that can help you to be an effective Leader. Now it's time to continue the Journey.

Question: Imagine that you have to decide between taking Option A or Option B – how do you know which to choose?

Answer: By knowing your Values.

For the purpose of this book, *a value is a quality that you have, or would like to have, that will help you to achieve your goals most effectively*. Values tend to be conceptual words – things that you cannot touch or hold for the most part, such as, love, creativity, power, freedom, wealth, time, family and so on. Values are usually collected subconsciously, and most often are based on the environment of one's upbringing. They are collected from parents, friends, family, society and from experiences as one grows. As the child becomes an adult, he or she defines their own values. They choose them, oftentimes, unbeknownst to them. Values shape the life we each live because they are being applied in our daily lives.

Values may change slightly over time and evolve we evolve. However, they are unlikely to change drastically over time unless a dramatic event occurs that modifies an individual's view of the world. An example of such an event can be death, separation or serious illness. Values rule how one interprets what is happening all around us at every moment, whether he or she knows it or not. Most people aren't aware that they are using their values to make decisions and frankly most people don't know their values. It's not because they don't know what makes them tick or happy, it's because most adults haven't had a values training or values identifier. I was one of those individuals. It wasn't until I started my Coaching firm full time, that I realized that college, corporate America, conferences I attended and/or the church, did not teach me about values or how to identify them. I was making decisions every day, not knowing why I'm making the decisions I'm making. After knowing my values and reflecting back at some past situations, that's when it dawned on me that it wasn't that the personalities were different, but it was the Values filter system that each party was using to respond was different. Knowing your values is such a critical part of our everyday life, because it impacts our feelings, which impact our actions, which becomes our results.

When you know your values, it is easier to know whether or not something is right for you, because your values are the things that are the most important to you – the things that you cannot live happily without. By knowing your values, you will be able to make decisions that you will find fulfilling and rewarding. By not knowing your values you make decisions that meet someone else's values and that's not good for you. Your values are your filtering system that you use when making decisions and that's why it's part of the laws of leadership, because decision making is one of the most important aspect of leadership.

Let's look at this from another perspective. Imagine that all of your favorite people in the world are together at one party with the sole purpose of celebrating you. At this party four different people, including a family member, a community member, a friend and a work colleague, make a speech about you. Take a few minutes to imagine what each person would say and write down the key concepts from each speech. Write down what you believe each person would say about you?

Speech 1 – given by a family member:

Speech 2 – given by someone from a community club or organization:

Speech 3 – given by a friend:

Speech 4 – given by a work colleague:

I imagine that each person that you have written all probably said something different about you. What should be consistent however, is that each of them should know what you stand for and what you believe in. Even though they may say slightly different things about you, fundamentally there should be a common language that they used to describe you. For example, anyone within the four speeches above that's describing me, would more than likely all say that she's the real deal. They probably would say that I am funny, live by principle, a leader, love family, celebrates life, and one that stands for justice and integrity and that I have a giving heart. Whether personally or professionally, these are typically what I hear people say about me, or what they perceive about me.

What they described are my Values. My top 10 values are, Family, Integrity, Time, Honesty, Trust, Fun, Spirituality, Health, Balance, and Authenticity. They are not in order of importance. I have my Values narrowed down to the top six and could probably even narrow them down to the top four, because I am crystal clear what they are, because I use them to make my decisions every day. Subsequently, it's important that you are able to begin to identify what your Values are. Values are more important than rules. They form mindsets and that can be good or bad, it all depends on what your Values are. Therefore, based on what you know about yourself and based on what I've shared in this chapter, I want you to take a moment and write down what you believe are your Top 10 Values. Your Values are your filtering system that you use to make your decisions and in order to be an effective and influential leader, you must be aware of what those values are. Please write down your Top 10 Values.

Top 10 Values

1. _____

_____

2. _____

_____

3. _____

_____

4. _____

_____

5. _____

_____

6. _____

_____

7. _____

_____

8. _____

_____

9. _____

_____

10. _____

_____

Being aware of your values will enable you to better understand:

- What motivates your actions

- The results you are getting in your life and why

- How to better resolve conflict

- How to live in a chaotic world

Conflict Resolution

"Conflict cannot survive without your participation."

Wayne Dyer

One of the benefits of knowing your Values and being sure of what they are and making sure that others know what you stand for is that it helps you to resolve conflicts in a more constructive way. Conflicts arise daily, it's a part of life. There will always be disagreements, misunderstandings, and strife. Some conflicts are healthy, and some can lead to serious consequences. It depends on what the conflict is all about and whether or not the parties are acting out of pure emotions and anger. It's only constructive when the conflict is between parties who know their Values.

I have coached and consulted so many individuals especially in the workplace, about how values directly affect their work life and home life. The success rate of our Values and Conflict Resolution Training remains at one-hundred percent **(100%)** because it's just that important to know your Values. The attendees leave feeling sure about themselves and their values. They become clearer about their path and understand why they do what they do. This training is one of my favorite ones to do because I know that most conflicts are a result of mis-understandings that can easily be resolved by understanding Values. We have helped organizations with employee retention, saving them hundreds of thousands of dollars, simply by conducting this training. I believe that there are many marriages that end in divorce because of the misunderstandings of values. Also, other relationships are tainted or destroyed for this same mis-understanding.

Most people mistake a value related issue with personality differences and attitude problems, when in reality the conflict arises because of each person's Values. He or she may be feeling disrespected or not being heard or of **no value**. Oftentimes, during conflicts one party or both may feel that the other person's personality is so different from there's or that there should be an attitude adjustment, and, in those cases, the argument leads nowhere.

The parties may become angry and sometimes these conflicts are so severe that they lead to physical altercations. Our Firm **have prevented so many great employees from quitting, being terminated** or getting themselves in serious trouble from the Values/Conflict Resolution Training that we offer.

Most conflicts and misunderstandings arise because of values being violated. Conflicts arise when values are so different that neither party can 'see' the other's person's point of view. An example is, in pre-marital counselling, our company coach engaged couples how to identify each of their individual top six values. If four of the top six values are not similar or identical, there will be a definite problem in that marriage.

The same if true in the workplace. When the leader and the team do not have similar values, there tends to be an increase in conflicts in the department. In our firm, we suggest to our Clients that part of the interview process (prior to being hired) is to conduct a values training. This will prevent employee turnover, hiring pitfalls and a dysfunctional working environment. More information about our training can be found at (www.carolynganderson.com), under the Consulting Tab.

ACTION STEPS!

TO DO!

Now that you have written down what you believe your **TOP 10 VALUES** are, it's time to narrow them down to your top six Values. Share this book (let them get their own) or this chapter with others that are connected to you and consider comparing your Values with theirs. You can conduct this exercise with your spouse, colleagues, family, friends or even the values of the place where you work and see it they are similar or quite different from yours. It may surprise you to see that some of the problems that you might have experienced or may be experiencing is because of your Values and how they differ from others. For any leader to be authentic, he or she must know what makes them tick. They must understand their convictions, what they stand for and what's their filtering system that he or she uses to make decisions daily. This is the definition of **VALUES**.

From your Top 10 Values, what would you consider to be your Top 6 Values? Write your Top 6 Values below (not based on order of importance).

Value #1

Value #2

Value #3

Value #4

Value #5

Value #6

Carry Your Values With You

Conscious awareness of your values enables you to make decisions and set priorities with ease. Write them in your journal, hang them in your bathroom and put them in your wallet.

Beliefs

Like values, your beliefs motivate you and also impacts the decisions that you make daily. You collect your beliefs, usually subconsciously, from your friends, family and society, and from your experiences. It is usually easier to radically change a belief than it is to radically change a value, because beliefs come from interpreting an event at a specific point in time. Beliefs are a feeling of certainty around what a thing means.

 EXAMPLE: Changing Values versus Changing Beliefs

It is harder to go from valuing 'health' to valuing 'illness,' and easier to go from believing that you are 'unfit' to believing that you are 'healthy.'

Beliefs can be totally empowering or totally disempowering (see example below). Most people are carrying around many disempowering beliefs that bring them down every day and they don't even know it.

EXAMPLE:

Disempowering Belief	Empowering Belief
I will never get ahead	I always learn something when I try something new
I always mess things up	

How many disempowering and empowering beliefs are you carrying around with you? Let's take a look at your beliefs and make sure that they all serve, support, nurture and challenge you.

"Whether you think you can or whether you think you can't, you are right."

Henry Ford

Exploring Beliefs

Explore some of your beliefs by completing the following sentences.

Note: 'They' could represent your family, work colleagues or friends. 'She/He' could represent someone who is important to you like you mother/father, daughter/son, sister/brother, friend, etc.

I always…

I never…

They are…

I can't…

We are…

My work is…

My time is…

My team is…

There are times when I…

Life is all about…

✎ *My beliefs:*

I love…

Success is…

Teamwork is…

Life is…

Family is…

Love is…

She can…

She is…

My parents are…

He could…

He is…

I am…

They are…

I can…

I can…

I can…

Empowering or Disempowering?

Take a few minutes to review your responses to each of the previous phrases. Write a 'D' next to each belief that is disempowering and an 'E' next to each belief that is empowering.

What does the previous exercise tell you about your beliefs?

What empowering beliefs do you have?

What can you replace your disempowering beliefs with?

NOTES..........

Journal the Journey – Notes from this Chapter

CHAPTER 3

LAW #3: GOALS AND DREAMS

 "If you want to live a happy life, tie it to a goal, not to people or things."

Albert Einstein

Life is a journey, and where we end up five, ten, or twenty years from now will be the direct result of the dreams that you dreamt and the goals that you set. Goals and Dreams and like Mission and Vision as described previously. Dreams are like your Vision, it is something that you see with your mind. It's something you ponder on, meditate on, and hope on. On the other hand, Goals are like your Mission, which are action items and taking steps. Goals have to be worked, just like your Mission. It is what you do and not necessarily what you see. Dreams and Goals go hand in hand. I teach my Coachee's how to activate their 24 Minutes Dream Moment daily, because without it, life can become a distraction.

Goals bring balance to your life and help you to arrange conflicting priorities in order of importance, while at the same time living life fully every day. If one doesn't have any Goals or Dreams, then there's nothing to look forward to. His or her life is being led by other people's goals and dreams.

To be an effective leader, goal setting must be a fundamental practice that he or she masters and that's why it's one of the Laws of Leadership. When constructing a house or a high-rise building, it is essential after laying the foundation to erect the support columns and frame the outer structure. These components should be built in such a way as to withstand shifting ground, wind, rain, water, etc.— because everything within the building relies on the stability of the infrastructure. So, shall Goals and Dreams be, they should be set in such a way that they support your Vision and Purpose.

Goal setting can be compared to creating a strong foundation and infrastructure—a process that shapes your dreams and ambitions, while giving you focus, discipline, resilience, and stability for the future. Having clear goals empowers your drive, fires your desires, and lights your passion so you can achieve any task, feat, voyage, or accomplishment that you aspire to do. Goals require action. It's one thing to have Goals written down, but they must be executed the right way and have timelines built into them, otherwise they will not work.

"People will judge you by your actions, not your intentions. You may have a heart of gold – but so does a hard-boiled egg."

Author Unknown

Goals must have a target date of accomplishment tied to them. You make your goals what you want them to be. No one can define your goals for you. It doesn't matter in what arena you work, whether you're an Entrepreneur, in public setting, education, business, the church, and/or government, setting goals help to shape your leadership and is one of the keys to success.

Your goals do not have to inspire anyone else except you. You should be the biggest fan of your goals and believe in them. No matter how big or small, they must ignite a fiery passion and speak to the greatness within, while also remaining congruent with your core values. According to Dr. Cindy Trimm, your goals must be both doable and achievable, so you can act with conviction in your pursuit of fulfillment and happiness—doing everything within your power to assure those goals are accomplished.

Goal Setting

Each January many put behind them the end of one year and celebrate the beginning of a new year. Many set (resolutions) which are supposed to be things that they will not do or people they will no longer see. These resolutions are normally negative in nature, such as "I will lose weight" versus, I will eat healthier and exercise each week. Instead of resolutions, one should be setting Goals, as resolutions are like wishes, and wishes are just that, a wish…a good intention with no destination.

There are several ways to set Goals and there are various models out there. One of the more popular model is the SMART Goals. I used the SMART Goals model earlier on when I started my consulting and coaching Firm. While I love the idea of having SMART Goals, I found that there were just a few more elements that helped me accomplished my goals that were not necessarily a part of the SMART Goals Model. This is why I have created my own model that many are using and have found it to work well. It's called the **S.T.R.O.N.G™** Goals Model.

The S.T.R.O.N.G™ Goals Model

The S.T.R.O.N.G™ Goals Model outlines some simple guidelines that you can use for setting effective goals in the key areas of your life.

S.T.R.O.N.G ™ stands for: Simple, Realistic, Opportunities, Network, Grow

- **S – Simple/Specific** Keep your Goals simple and focused, rather than wordy and vague. Be very specific about the outcome you want.

- **T – Time** This is the **BIG ONE!** Time is essential, and you can only use it effectively, as it cannot be managed. There's no such thing as time management. The sun rises when it wants to, and it goes down when it wants to. You cannot stop time; therefore, it cannot be managed. With that being said, there are three specific ways that you need to write your Time when setting Goals. They are as follows:

  1. Set specific time each day when you will FOCUS on you and your Goals.

  2. Give your goals a specific due date

  3. State your goal as if it's already been achieved. For example, if one of your goals is to be debt

free by a certain year, say 2024. You would write the Time as such: It is the year 2024 and I am Debt Free. This trains the unconscious mind to accept the goal as real, which helps you to move more effectively towards it. Set timeframes for all your goals.

- **R – Realistic & Resilience** The goal must be achievable, and you must make up in your mind that you will **FOCUS** and not STOP until you achieve your Goals.

- **O – Opportunities & Options** Show up to places that will give you opportunities to achieve your Goal/s. List 2 or 3 different options to achieve these Goals. Give yourself some flexibility and choices. If one way doesn't work, then do it the other way.

- **N – Network leads to NET-WORTH** Connect to the right people and create your right circle. Being a part of a network that truly believes in you and desires to see you prosper is the best thing for you to achieve your Goals and this will lead to your net-worth. People buy products, products don't buy products, so you will always want to have a solid network of people that are investing in you and you are investing in them. Network is a relationship and should not be one-sided. It should be mutually beneficial.

- **G – Give & GROW** If you ever want to achieve your Goals & Dreams one must GIVE. It's the law of sowing and reaping. When you give (time, money, energy etc.), you are guaranteed to reap. How little time you give to achieve your Goals will be the same level that you reap. Spend your time wisely and use it effectively so that you can succeed and GROW.

Goal setting is an intricate part of being of re-building the pillars of leadership. Goals are needed in all areas of life. Whether personally or professionally. Goals are what major corporations use to be profitable, to design new products, to expand into new territories and to build their brand. This book is a result of a Goal that was set. I had timelines built into writing this book. I knew that if I wanted it to be published at a certain time, then it was necessary for me to finish writing within a certain timeframe. To lead well, you need Goals.

NOTES..........

Journal the Journey – Notes from this Chapter

NOTES..........

Journal the Journey – Notes from this Chapter

CHAPTER 4

LAW #4: SKILLS, TRAITS AND COMPETENCIES

"A winner is someone who recognizes his God-given talents, works his tail off to develop them into skills, and uses these skills to accomplish his goals."

Larry Bird

Skills

Usain Bolt, born August 21, 1986, affectionately known as Lightning Bold, is today, as of the first publishing of this book, the world's fastest man in the world. What many may not know is that Bolt experienced some set-backs and failures before being a world champion. He wasn't always as fast as he is, and he also didn't always win his races. So, how did he become the world's fastest man, when during some early races, there was someone else that was faster that the Lighting himself? How is this possible?

Born in the beautiful island of Jamaica (such as myself), there were certain skills and talent that seemed to come naturally. One of those skills is the ability to run with speed. Jamaicans are known for their speed when it comes to track and field. One of the reasons I can attribute to this notion, is because mostly everywhere that Jamaicans had to go (especially before having personal cars) we had to walk. Even though there were taxi's available, they were mostly filled up by the time it got to you.

Personally, I recall walking to school, church, grocery store, beach, and pretty much everywhere. I am not talking about a few feet. I am talking about miles upon miles, and looking back now, it seemed like nothing. I don't even like walking from a distant parking space into the store. I drive around and around until I find a close spot. Yes, I know I should find the furthest parking space, but don't judge me. I've done my share of walking, furthermore where I live for most of my life, was not on the tropics of Jamaica but in the cold Midwest, where 11 of the 12 months of the year are cold. Okay...moving on.... Thus, using the legs were second nature to Jamaicans.

Consequently, track and field, soccer and various types of sports that uses speed and legs started very early for most Jamaicans. Track and Field races and competitions started as early as first grade, if not before. The minute a child realizes that he or she has legs, they start using them to play and race. I can imagine this was the case for Lightning Bolt. He probably started racing and running at a very early age and participated in the annual sports events that is held at every primary (elementary) school that I knew of in Jamaica. Just like July 4th celebration in the United States, Sports Day was the same big deal. There were vendors, and community cheers, races, prizes, food and games. It was simple spectacular.

During Bolt's early years as a sprinter, soccer and cricket player, his speed was noticed by coaches at the school he attended. As early as age 14, Bolt was wowing fans by sprinting with his lightning speed. He won his first high school championship medal in 2001 but received a silver medal in the 200-meter race This meant that someone else won the gold-medal. Another person at the time was faster than Bolt. (https://www.biography.com/people/usain-bolt-20702091).

There were other occasions where Bolt didn't win his race. In 2007, Bolt broke the national 200-meter record held for over 30 years by Donald Quarrie and earned two **silver** medals at the World Championship in Osaka, Japan. He took back the 100-meter world title on August 11, 2013, after having lost the title in 2011.

In May 2015, Bolt faced some challenges. He came in second at the Nassau IAAF World Relays https://www.biography.com/people/usain-bolt-20702091. He was also plagued with a hamstring injury that would affect him over and over again. Several sprinters have this problem. I've had my share of pulled hamstring injuries when I ran track and field in high school. Nevertheless, this didn't stop Bolt from pursuing his career. Even though Bolt had natural talent and abilities, it still required work to enhance his skill.

Tweet

"Greatness is just right around the corner for he or she who works toward developing their skills"

Dr. Carolyn

Bolt and his coaching team and mentors worked tirelessly to develop his skill and to push him to the limit without recurring injuries. During what some called off-season, it was on-season for Bolt. He nurtured and improved upon his skills of speed, agility, stride, sportsmanship, days upon days upon days, and that extra drive was what afforded him to be called the world's fastest man.

This in essence is the definition of Skills and Competencies. Greatness is just right around the corner for he or she who works towards developing their skills. No matter what field of work one is in, whether in Business, Education, Media, Church, Government,

Healthcare, Family, Technology, Sports, Arts & Entertainment, and so on, in order to win and be successful in life, the skills must be developed and worked on. To win at leadership, work on your skills.

Even though I knew I was a great Speaker and it came naturally for me, I still had to work on the art of developing my skills and abilities to remain proficient. So, did Bolt. After working on his **skills**, he ended up winning three gold medals at the 2008 Olympic Games in Beijing, China, and becoming the first man in Olympic history to win both the 100-meter and 200-meter races in record times. Bolt also won three Olympic gold medals at the 2012 Summer Olympic Games in London. He ran the men's 100-meter race in 9.63 seconds, a new Olympic record, making him the first man in history to set three world records in Olympic competition, (https://www.biography.com/people/usain-bolt-20702091).

He made history again at the 2016 Summer Games in Rio when he won gold in the 100-meter and 200-meter race and 4x100-meter relay, completing a "triple-triple," earning three gold medals at three consecutive Olympics for a total of 9 gold medals over the course of his Olympic career.

This is what Skills is all about. Bolt knew his weaknesses, his strengths, the threats he faced and the opportunities he had. Once he focused on perfecting his skills, it paid off BIG TIME for him. Forbes magazine estimated in June 2017 that Bolt is worth about $34.2 million dollars. Maybe I should have worked on my running skills a little bit more (lol). https://www.biography.com/people/usain-bolt-20702091

 ACTION STEPS!

TO DO!

S.W.O.T Analysis

Part of understanding where you are as a Leader and what competencies, skills or traits you will need to become the best you, it's good to have a SWOT Analysis Self-Assessment. I love doing SWOT Analysis because it keeps me grounded and humbled and aware of my strengths and areas of opportunities. Being consciously aware means walking through life awake, with eyes open and mind alert. This means noticing the relationship between actions and results and continually thinking about different ways to get the results you seek. Sometimes you will get it right and sometimes you won't. In both instances you learn, grow and move forward. Subsequently, that's why it's important to do a personal SWOT Analysis. SWOT stands for Strengths, Weaknesses, Opportunities and Threats. You can utilize this analysis technique to make an informed decision on how to move forward for almost any situation you may find yourself in or any area of your life.

What would you consider to be some of your Strengths? What are you good at? What are skills that you know emphasizes your strengths?

What would you consider to be your Weaknesses? What are you not good at? What are some skills that are missing from your life?

What would you consider to be areas of Opportunities? What are some things you can work on to master it? What needs a little tweaking?

What would you consider to be some Threats? Are there any behavior's, attitudes, traits that are affecting your growth and progress in life? Are there any mistakes that you keep repeating?

Let's narrow it down to a very specific situation. Think of a current situation, state of mind, season or space that you are in right now. In the box below, list:

- The strengths you have that will help you overcome the situation
- Any weaknesses that may get in your way moving forward
- Any current opportunities waiting to be grabbed
- Any possible threats that should be considered

My Strengths	My Weaknesses

Current Opportunities	Possible Threats

For any area of your life, business or career, you can use this simple SWOT Analysis as a spot check to evaluate where you are in life. It's an effective tool that can be used to determine what skills you have to succeed, or any competencies that you need to acquire. Effective Leaders must always be aware of their current circumstances and state of mind, so that he or she can make constructive decisions. Reality checks are needed continuously.

What are the Strengths you listed above?

What would you consider the Weaknesses?

What about areas of Opportunities?

What about Threats? What attitude, idea, mindset, etc., are considered threats as it relates to that situation?

Traits

"Traits like humility, courage, and empathy are easily overlooked – but is immensely important to find them in your closest relationships."

Laura Linney

Derek Anthony Redmond, born September 3, 1965 is a retired British athlete. He was a really good athlete and worked very hard for all his accomplishments in the sport of Track and Field. During his career, he held the British record for the 400 meters race and also won gold medals in the 4x400 meters relay at the World Championships, European Championships, and the Commonwealth Games.

Like most athletes, Derek's career included a series of injuries. Any sport that requires lots of movement, especially with speed, tends to have a higher rate of injury than others. This was the case for Derek. In the 1992 Olympic Games in Barcelona, Derek was placed in lane five (5) as he prepared to run the 400 meters semi-final race. He had worked so hard to get to this level of the competition, because one of the highest accomplishments for most athletes is to participate at the Olympics. I said most, because I am or was an athlete, and ran that same race as Derek. I also did the long jump, triple jump, 4x100 meter relay and the 4x200 meter relay and was good at it. I also won gold medals, a few silver medals and enjoyed the sport of Track and Field. However, it was never my desire to make it to the Olympics, perhaps because I didn't see myself racing (running) professionally.

Derek took his start and at the sound of the gun, he shot out of the blocks and was on pace to be one of the top finishers of the semi-final race. After completing the first 100 meters, he was striding along and suddenly, out of nowhere, Derek fell to the ground. I can only imagine the various thoughts that flooded Derek's mind and the spectators. Why did Derek fell to the ground?

Devastatingly and unfortunately, Derek had incurred a runner's worst nightmare, a torn hamstring. I know, I've experienced a torn hamstring, in the midst of a race. With tears running down his eyes and the look of agony on his face, Derek stood up and began limping on one leg as he was determined to reach the finish line. The track and field officials attempted to help him off the field, but Derek shrugged them off as he limped closer to the finish line. Derek knew that he had to finish what he started, because that's what leaders do. He knew that he couldn't let an injury, or what appears to be a failure, stopped him from finishing. He knew that it wasn't about the title that he's not getting or have won before, but it was about how he would respond. True leadership is more than a title it's a behavior.

As Derek continued his limping to the finish line, it appeared that something else was going on. There seemed to be rumblings in the stands. There was a man who was pressing his way through the crowd and was making his way to the field where Derek was. He leaped over the fence, passing by the officials as they attempted to stop him, but he was determined to reach Derek. It was Derek's father, racing to the side of his son who had worked all his life to achieve his goal by being a part of the Olympics. He had seen Derek take leadership of his life as he worked tirelessly to achieve a goal. He knew what his son had been through. When he got to him, he held Derek and placed Derek's hand over his shoulder and together they made their way to the finish line to the cheers and standing ovation of the crowd. What a story!

This evidence of leadership, perseverance and will-power has become a well-remembered moment in Olympic history and has left a lasting impression of never giving up. Derek may have lost the race that day, but he and his father left the stadium winners. While Derek worked on his skills to be a better runner, it was his innate **trait** of perseverance that caused him to limp across the finish line.

Tweet

"Skills may slow you down, but Traits pick you up"

Dr. Carolyn

Skills may slow you down, but traits pick you up and let you keep going. Derek and his father displayed that true leadership is about never giving up and fighting to the very end. Even if one has to limp to finish the race, then that is what is necessary to get the job done. Leadership is about perseverance. It's about not backing down, it's about having a made-up mind that win or lose, be steadfast, unmovable to lead with dignity and honor. Both Derek and his father showed that you can win, simply by persevering.

Source: http://brainprick.com/derek-redmond-it-doesnt-matter-how-hard-it-is-but-you-must-finish-what-you-started/

In the previous section, we discussed about skills that are necessary for effective leadership and how to use those skills to maximize one's purpose. While skills are something that can be acquired and improved on, such as what Usain Bolt did and other leaders such as Michael Jordan who was cut from his high school basketball team but decided to improve his skills and eventually rose to be one of the world's greatest basketball player, **traits** operate differently. Traits are really something that's more innate, even though they can be worked on, but not as easily as skills. It was Derek's trait of perseverance, persistency and a winning attitude that took him across the finish line. He could have stayed on the field, cried all day and rest in his pain. He would have had every right to do that, because one could only imagine what he was going through internally. He had developed his skills, worked on his injuries and made it to the championship game, only to not be able to finish the race because of an injury. Surely, he had to have been quite disappointed. He would have been within reason to just lay on the field and weep, but he didn't. The traits that he embodied would not allow him to do give up.

According to Collins Dictionary, "a trait is a particular characteristics, quality, or tendency that someone or something has" (www.collinsdictionary.com). Merriam Webster further defines a trait as "a distinguishing quality; an inherited characteristic" (www.merriam-webster.com). There are certain traits that authentic, effective, positive leaders should embody. Many people claim they are a leader, yet, they do not exhibit the necessary tools, personality, or traits to lead. That becomes apparent when projects fail, or things don't turn out the way as planned and rather than accepting responsibly, he or she blames, deflects or ignore the matter. That's when the traits of passivity or aggression kicks in.

An effective leader should have certain skills and traits. Traits like honestly, integrity, persistence, drive and so forth, should come naturally for leaders. I believe that the debate about whether leaders are born or can be made stems from the lack of having certain traits. Certain traits come naturally for some leaders and for others they need to be developed. I believe that leaders are both born and can be made. Sometimes leaders have natural leadership traits but require training and/or coaching to develop the trait or just to be aware that it exist. This is also the benefit of values training as mentioned in a previous chapter. A leader must have skills and traits to accomplish goals, live out the vision and walk out the mission, whether personally or professionally.

Amongst the many leadership traits that an effective leader should have, being results driven and solutions-based rank at a very high percentage. Leaders should have a pretty good idea about the outcome of any project or goal. It's one of the natural traits of a leader. It's one thing to have multiple meetings and great conversations, but if they are not producing fruit or results driven, it's pointless. Leadership should be solutions based. Trust is another trait that leaders should naturally have. Unfortunately, leadership today is lacking trust. It appears that so many people do not trust those in leadership roles. That is why this book is so important as it can be used as a guide to rebuild the fundamental principles, characteristics and mindsets of what leadership is all about. Earth is mourning and groaning for the re-birth of authentic leadership. It's longing for leaders with natural traits that can turn a failing world into a thriving one, because they care and love the people they serve. Are you one of the turn-around leaders?

Traits can be good, or they can be bad. Common Traits that Leaders should have or not are:

The 10 Must Haves:

1. Perseverance

2. Integrity

3. Confidence

4. Drive

5. Tenacity

6. Vulnerability

7. Compassion

8. Love

9. Peace

10. Clarity

The 10 Have Nots:

1. Bad attitude

2. Pride

3. Selfishness

4. Impatience

5. Passivity

6. Un-focused

7. Hatred

8. Lies

9. Greed

10. Defeating persona

NOTES...........

Journal the Journey – Notes from this Chapter

NOTES..........

Journal the Journey – Notes from this Chapter

CHAPTER 5

LAW #5: THE GENERATIONS
THE GENERATIONAL DIFFERENCES

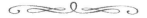

"Live a Legacy, Leave a Legacy"

K.Anthony

"Why do you want to re-locate your business to Chiraq or even start a Talk Show here?" the interviewer asked me. It was the first time I heard the name Chiraq, which when explained is a combination of Chicago and Iraq. This is the nickname that has been given to America's third largest city according to urbandictionary.com. They further explained that the reason for the nickname was because more murders have occurred in Chicago that during the war in Iraq. That's quite astonishing. I can understand why she would want to know why I would want to be identified with a city as such, considering that there is a mass exodus of African Americans that are leaving the city. My response to her, was that "Chicago was the city of wealth and that I was going to do everything to showcase the greatest that's in the city." She sighed as to say, "okay Madame."

Born on April 16, 1993 as Chancelor Johnathan Bennett, this Chicago native is not focusing on Chiraq, but rather creating his own world. Chiraq is not a focal point for the Millennial-more like a border line Centennial, also known as **Chance the Rapper**. He has done what most Generation X would probably not do and that is going out on a limb and doing something that hasn't been done before.

Generation Xer's tend to wait on permission to take a step and sometimes will lose out on opportunities, because of that characteristic. Chance the Rapper does not have a record deal and most of his profits comes from live streaming. In fact, he's the only artist to earn a Grammy award solely from streaming (https://www.biography.com/people/chance-the-rapper-5152017). This is one of the leadership traits of a Generation Y (Millennials), they take risks and don't wait for permission before making a move. They are also the most talked about Generation, not because they are more in numbers, but because folks tend to refer to all youth as Millennials', when at times they are actually Centennials.

Different generations lead differently. There are some characteristics that shapes and define how each generation view leadership or even their leadership styles. This is not everyone within the generations, but the majority. Surely, there are outliers that don't necessarily fit into any category. For example, a Baby Boomer born and raised on a farm in a rural town and one that was born and raised in New York City will more than likely have very different viewpoints, values, and outlook on life. In actuality, they don't even have to be born in two different states to be so different, it can be within the same small island and yet be different.

While writing the last few chapters of this book in Panama City Beach, I met a fellow Jamaican and I was sharing with her how much I love the resort and the beach. She replied, "I don't like it." I said why? She said, "she's from Kingston, Jamaica where there's lots of comradery, and Panama City Beach is the opposite." I said, "I bet you like New York." Oh, my goodness, her face lit up and she said, "I love New York!" For her childhood, a typical day is lots of action, hustle, movement, fast pace and lots going on, and for me, it was the Ocean breeze, calm and peaceful, just like Panama City Beach, Florida. My point is, we are products of our environment and oftentimes it affects our leadership styles. While the descriptions may not be for everyone within the different groups, for the most part, they're pretty accurate and the majority rules, per se.

Here is the breakdown of the Generations

Name	Years	Age – in 2018	Timespan
Traditionalist	Born 1945 and before	73 years and older	
Baby Boomer	Born 1946 to 1964	54 - 72 Years Old	18 years
Generation X	**Born 1965 to 1976**	42-53 Years Old	11 years
Generation Y (Millennials)	Born 1977 to 1995	23-41 Years Old	18 years
Generation Z Centennials	Born 1996 to 2017	1-22 Years Old	21 Years

The Newly Created Generation

Generation E **(Remnants)** Enlightenment Eighteen Empowered Eclipse iPhone Eight	Born 2018 to 2036		18 Years

Generation E is the newly created generation that I have established, because there needs to be a new one. The timespan for Generation Z – the Centennials has reached its mature timespan surpassing 18 years. The generational timespan are usually 18 years with the exception of Generation X, with only and 11-year timespan. They were X'd out of the picture and cut short to introduce the Millennials to the world – I guess. Gen-Xers didn't even get a chance to reach puberty, much less teenagers. The Y's (why are they here, lol), took over, which is actually one of their traits, which I will discuss later.

Things are getting ready to change for the Gen Xer's, because they are the greatest leaders for today. They were born with natural leadership traits and because most had to learn the hard way, they know what it takes to establish themselves and also to be true overcomers which is a trait of great leadership. They are also patient, understand tenacity, great helpers, and are ready to have their turn. Generation X, are the only generation that cannot reproduce within its generation. What I mean by that is, a Baby Boomer, could be the parent of another Baby Boomer, same for Millennials and Centennials, considering that an 18-year-old or younger teenager can have a child. Not so, for Generation X. It's very unlikely for an eleven (11) year old child to have had a child. If there are, it's not the majority.

It's very important to understand the strengths, weaknesses, opportunities, threats, of the various generations as it helps to communicate how each age group think, act, and view leadership. When you're aware of these behaviors, it closes the gap for potential conflicts and mis-understandings. Awareness creates understanding and once you understand why others do what they do and the reason for it, or even why you are the way you are, it makes life so much easier.

As a college professor of older Centennials, Millennials, some Generation X and Baby Boomers, it was like being a teacher to different sets of students from different worlds. The traditional day time students between the ages of 18-24 gave me a hard time. It took them awhile to settle down in class and their attention span was maybe three minutes tops. I spent more time going over their homework that they should have done, and going through all the various excuses, than time used for teaching.

The non-traditional students who were mostly working adults and/or parents and were in class with me for four (4) hours per night were so different. They were focused and serious about their school work. They didn't have a lot of excuses why they didn't do their work, because they actually did their homework. Most of them were Gen X and Baby Boomers, who probably put their college life on hold to raise their children. The discussions during class time were very healthy and constructive and the students looked forward to learning from each other. They were excited for the opportunity just to be in college. It's as though they looked forward to being back in school. I used different languages when communicating with each group. I had studied the generations for so long that I was able to effectively communicate with each group in their own language.

History of the Generations

Meet the Traditionalist Generation

Traditionalist	Born 1945 and before	73 years and older

During this generation, a total of 55 million people was born between 1925 - 1946. This generation grew up during the Great Depression and World War II. During this time period, this generation either fought during World War II or were children. This generation is also known as the "Silent Generation" due to the fact that they were seen but not heard. The generation was described as unimaginative, withdrawn, unadventurous and cautious.

Strengths

- Wealthiest generation

- Largest voting population

- Team players

- Possessed superb interpersonal skills

- The happiest generation in America

Weaknesses

- Behavior based on the experiences from the Great Depression

- Wanted to feel needed

- Low self esteem

Opportunities

- Has largest lobbyist group, AARP

- Understood the nobility of sacrifice for the common good

- Demand for new industries (increased demand for airplanes and weaponry) brought economic recovery

- During this generation and because of the Great Depression and WWII, it redefined the government's role in society and developed America into the worlds' most powerful country

- Adopted the overall culture, art and music of the previous generation, the G.I. Generation (people born between 1901 – 1924)

Threats

- The Cold War

- McCarthyism – The House Committee on Un-American Activities launched an assault on political freedom in America and Senator Joseph McCarthy overzealous attempts to feed anti-communist sentiment in America, making it dangerous for people to speak freely about their opinions and beliefs.

- The Dust Bowl (dust storms) swept the country and destroyed farmlands, which resulted in starvation

Sources:

https://study.com/academy/lesson/the-silent-generation-definition-characteristics-facts.html

http://www.marstoncomm.com/matures.html;http://merrillassociates.com/

Meet the Baby Boomers

Baby Boomer	Born 1946 to 1964	54 - 72 Years Old	18 years

During this generation, a total of 76 million people was born between 1946 - 1964. This generation grew up during the Civil Rights Movement and the Cold War. This generation was known as the "Empty Nesters." This generation was born during a spike in child births after WWII, which named them the "Baby Boomers." Four million babies were born each year between 1953 – 1964. They believed the following regarding working: a) work ethic is measured in hours worked b) teamwork is critical to success c) relationship building is important and d) they expect loyalty from those they work with.

Strengths

- The largest generation
- Largest workforce
- Free-Spirited
- Financially secure and consumer oriented

Weaknesses

- Believed rules should be obeyed unless they are contrary to what they want, and then the rules are to be broken

- Experimental

- Individualism

- Did not mentor Generation X

Opportunities

- Created the term workaholic

- Civil Rights Women's and Environmental Movements

- Self-discovery

- Mothers did not have to work anymore and was able to return home and take care of their families

- Increase of suburban living (buying up of land on the outskirts of major cities and building houses)

- Credit Cards were introduced

- Redefined Religion

Threats

- Cold War

- Vietnam War

- Protests and Sit-Ins

- Assassination of JFK, Robert Kennedy and Martin Luther King, Jr.

Sources:

https://study.com/academy/lesson/the-silent-generation-definition-characteristics-facts.html and

http://www.marstoncomm.com/matures.html;http://merrillassociates.com/;

http://www.escapehomes.com/articles/Baby_Boomers_Statistics_on_Empty_Nests_and_Retirement.htm

Meet Generation X

Generation X	**Born 1965 to 1976**	42-53 Years Old	11 years

During this generation, a total of 50 million people was born between 1965 - 1980. Generation X are the descendants of "The Baby Boomer" generation and they precede Generation Y, known as the "Millennials." This generation were defined as "slackers." Their philosophies are: a) work smarter and not harder, b) casual, friendly work environment, c) a place to learn, d) prefer open communication regardless of position, title or tenure and e) value of time.

Strengths

- First generation to develop ease and comfort with technology

- Independent

- Self-Reliant

- Entrepreneurial

- Multi-taskers

- Value Family time

Weaknesses

- "X" described the lack of identity that members of Generation X felt, not sure where they belong

- Had to learn to fend for themselves

- Quest for emotional security

- Reject rules

Opportunities

- The rise of computers and video games

- Birth of the internet

- Fall of Berlin Wall

- Development of Reality TV (MTV Show)

Threats

- More Divorces than any other generation

- Rise of HIV and AIDS

- Watergate

- This generation created a "latchkey" environment, where the children came home while the parents where still at work, which resulted in Generation X taking care of themselves.

- The Chernobyl disaster

- The Persian Gulf War

- September 11, 2011 attack of the World Trade Center

Sources:

https://study.com/academy/lesson/the-silent-generation-definition-characteristics-facts.html

http://www.marstoncomm.com/matures.html;
http://merrillassociates.com/;
http://apps.americanbar.org/lpm/lpt/articles/mgt08044.html

Meet Generation Y – Millennials

Generation Y (Millennials)	Born 1977 to 1995	23-41 Years Old	18 years

Generation Y are connected, diverse collaborators, and most definitely shaped by 9/11. There are roughly 80 million Millennials. According to Brain Science, there is no such thing as multitasking, but Millennials can switch from task to task quite quickly. They are also engaged in politics more than previous generations. Not only taking but creating new pathways to new ways to do things in life.

Strengths

- Optimistic

- Technology native

- Diversity

- Multitaskers

- Expectation to always succeed

- When one plan falls through, there will be a back-up plan

Weaknesses

- Contradictions

- Go with the flow

- Need things done right now and not later

- ADD/ADHD & Anxiety medications prescribed at an all-time high

- Extremely high student loan debt

Opportunities

- Personal branding

- Using technology for new focus directions

- Could focus more

Threats

- Absent technology driven aspects

- In Debt

- Want everything right now

- Inpatient

- Overly Zealous

- Can be disrespectful

- Being told NO!

- Hovering parents

Sources:

"The Millennial Generation Research Review." *U.S. Chamber of Commerce Foundation*, 15 Mar. 2017, www.uschamberfoundation.org/reports/millennial-generation-research-review.

Meet Generation Z – Centennials

Generation Z Centennials	Born 1996 to 2017	1-22 Years Old	21 Years

Generation Z, are technologically driven. They have never known a life without technology such as, smart phones and gaming systems. They like to fix their problems using a technological gadget, even at a young age. Gen Z's are exposed to sexuality and porn due to access on the internet.

Strengths

- Drug use, alcohol consumption, teenage pregnancy is at an all-time low.

- Develop unique products

- Provide visual depths in different ways

- Working in groups, whether local or across the globe

Weaknesses

- Conversations in person

- Attention span of 8 seconds

- Does not like change

Opportunities

- Wanting to change the world with social media aspects

- More than likely to work in technology fields rather than people interactive environments

- Propose challenges for older generations on their knowledge of all information sources

Threats

- Face to face interaction

- Tasks that have a change of course action

- Being told that something is not possible (they have the drive to prove them wrong)

Sources:

"The Millennial Generation Research Review." *U.S. Chamber of Commerce Foundation*, 15 Mar. 2017, www.uschamberfoundation.org/reports/millennial-generation-research-review.

Meet Generation E – Remnants - Enlightenment

Generation E	Born 2018 to 2036	Conception,	18 Years
Remnants		Infants,	
Enlightenment		Developing (at the time of	
Eighteen		writing this book,	
Empowered		2018)	
Eclipse			

I would like to introduce you to Gen E – they are the beginning of the Enlightenment Generation and the ones who will probably see and experience technological advances like never before. Their parents can be any of the preceding generations, except the Traditionalists, even though Sarah in the bible had her first child at age ninety (90) and Abraham her husband was ninety-nine (99). Therefore, anything is possible.

Generation E, will get to experience a historic Eclipse in 2024 and the introduction of more drones, holograms, Astra-projections and the expansion of robotic innovations. The world from their point of view will be and look quite different from what it is for the Centennials that are closer in age to the Millennials. I am excited about this Generation, because they will get to partake in the new paradigm shift for Leadership and the restoration of Leaders that lead with high morals, are purpose-driven, visionaries and honest. Hopefully, I will be alive to live out the eighteen years with them, as I hope to be one of the Leaders that help to train and guide them in the right direction. Here are my SWOT predictions for Gen E.

Strengths

- Wealthy

- Innovative

- Team players

- Confident

- Respectful

- Creative

Weaknesses

- Lack verbal communication

- Entitlement

- Anxiety

- Lack financial acumen

Opportunities

- Be great leaders

- Change how young people are viewed

- Demonstrate the need for a human interaction workforce

- Influencers

Threats

- Replace by Robots (workforce)

- Anti-social (personally)

- A.D.D.

- Immoral

What have you learned about the Traditionalist and what did the synopsis of their SWOT say to you about how they lead?

What have you learned about the Baby Boomers and what did the synopsis of their SWOT say to you about how they lead?

What have you learned about the Generation X and what did the synopsis of their SWOT say to you about how they lead?

What have you learned about the Generation Y and what did the synopsis of their SWOT say to you about how they lead?

What have you learned about the Generation Z and what did the synopsis of their SWOT say to you about how they lead?

What are your thoughts about Generation E?

Age Differences

Understanding and knowing about the various generations is key to understanding how leadership varies amongst different groups. While it does not necessarily describe everyone within the generations, I believe it speaks true for the majority. It helps to understand why certain people think the way they do and since this book is about re-establishing the fundamental principles of leadership, it's needed.

Our Firm does a lot of training on Conflict Resolution and what we have found is that the conflicts arise from mis-understanding and mis-judgement (besides values differences, mentioned before). In some organizations, the managers are the recent college graduates and the staff that reports to them are more advanced in years and oftentimes have been with company for over 20 years. The older generation find it difficult to adhere to what the younger generation is saying or wanting them to do and the younger generation are taking the stance of "I'm the manager," in essence, do as I say.

Going even deeper, not only are there generational differences, but also age differences. Most of the generational age ranges are 18-21-year span, except for Generation X, who's timespan is only 11 years. I am sure that a seven (7) year old Centennials thinks differently than a seventeen (17) year old

Centennial (Generation Z). Their brains are in different developmental stages.

Therefore, in an effort to add more depth to the age groups, I have broken down the Generations even further into smaller age brackets. I like to refer to this as the **Age-Grid**. One of my goals for this book, is to have us understand each other better. This will help to bring more unity, peace and content in our lives. Much of the chaos today can be resolved if we just understand each other.

Age Grid

0 - 10 - Age of Absorbing, Learning, Needing, Shaping,

11 - 19 - Age of Puberty, Molding, Maturing, Learning, Rebelling

20 - 20's - Age of Exploring – Experiencing – Deciding

30 - 30's - Age of Understanding and Committing

40 - 40's - Age of Purpose & Meaning

50 - 50's - Age of Establishment

60 - 60's - Age of Elegance (Woman) & Dignity/Valor (Male)

70 - 70's - Age of Favor

80 - 80's - Age of Blessings & Mercy

90 - 90's - Age of Fulfillment

100 - 119 - Age of Peace

120 – on - Age of Promise

Which Age Category do you fall on the grid? According to the description of that category what does it say about you? Can you relate to it? How does this help you to be a more effective leader?

_____

_____

_____

_____

_____

_____

_____

_____

_____

_____

_____

I hope that you are starting to understand yourself a little more, as it's important to be confident in who you are, so that you can lead authentically.

Personality Styles

Am I a Sapphire, Ruby, Emerald or Pearl personality type? I've heard others say they are type A, and yet others a different type. Where do these types come from? So far, I've shared with you about the different generations, then the age grid and now we're narrowing it down to the Personality Styles, which are different from personality traits. Traits are more like perseverance, drive, passion, endurance and so forth. These are traits that leaders should have in order to be an effective leader. Moving beyond the scope of traits, are the different personality types.

There are several products on the market that focuses on different personality types. Some of them are great and some are weird, or the politically correct term is different. However, I have found one that works so well and is such a profound example of true differences amongst personality styles, and since I didn't want to re-invent the wheel that already exist, I have adopted, purchased, and use Dani Johnson's personality styles that she calls GEMS®. Dani Johnson is one of my mentors and she is just an extraordinary woman and I give her credit for her concepts, ideas and leadership. I relate very well to her, because we have quite a few similarities, such as how we think about different things. When I attend any of her conferences, I like when she does the GEMS® Training. We are products of some of her teachings and she consider it a delight when the principles that she teaches are being applied.

GEMS®

In the GEMS® Mastery personality model, Dani says that there are four different personality categories, namely; Sapphire, Pearl, Emerald and Ruby, thus the word gems. Here are her descriptions of the various personality types.

SAPPHIRES

- Are motivated by fun!

When Approaching SAPPHIRES

- Be upbeat and friendly

- Smile, Smile, Smile!

- Give an energetic handshake

- Keep things simple

- Build rapport

- Let them talk

- Don't be arrogant

- Show then your fun side

- They are attracted to positive people

- Good, yet warm eye contact

Identifying a SAPPHIRE In The Audience

- Ask engaging questions: "Wouldn't it be great if…"
- Keep the communication interactive
- Keep them engaged in the process
- Keep your pace of speech fairly quick, this helps keep them engaged
- Make it entertaining
- Always keep it positive
- Offer humor whenever it is applicable
- Keep it simple
- Use easy language – keep it conversational and not too serious
- Tell stories and/ or show pictures

PEARLS

- Are motivated by a cause (usually teachers, humanitarians)

When Approaching PEARLS

- Be courteous
- Be relational

- Keep your time of voice a bit softer

- Ask them questions to get them to share information

- Give a soft handshake with both hands

- Be an attentive listener

- Don't be pushy

- Share your caring/ nurturing side (Yes, all GEMS® have this to a degree)

- Good, yet informal eye contact

- They are attracted to people who are giving

Identifying a Pearl In The Audience

- Begin by relating to them

- Be very open with them

- Slow your pace of speech down a bit

- Don't become over-excited; this overwhelms them

- Share personal stories of how others have been helped by using your service/ product /idea

- Be real: Pearl can feel it if you are being false and will not trust you

- Tell stories and or show pictures

EMERALDS

- Are motivated by facts and figures

When Approaching an EMERALDS

- Respect their time

- Be a professional

- Give a quick but firm handshake

- Respect their personal space – don't be a close talker

- Ask them more specific questions to really get them to talk to you

- Don't be a chatter box

- Answer their questions directly when appropriate

- Show them the process

- Validate that it works

- They are attracted to people with a system to complete tasks and get results

- Have good eye contact that is direct and focused

Identifying A Pearl In The Audience

- Be very detailed in your conversations

- Use statistics and figures when applicable

- Explain the "why" questions; example: "You may be thinking, 'Well why is that necessary?' Let me explain."

- Explain the solutions

- Focus on what steps to take

- Be very thorough – the more information they have the more comfortable they feel

- Show them how to get any further questions answered

RUBIES

- Are motivated by a challenge and/ or money

Approaching RUBIES

- If face-to-face, "dress to impress"

- Be very confident

- Have a strong stance

- Give a strong and firm handshake

- Look them in the eye

- Approach the situation with a result in mind

- Compliment them and mean it

- Tell them success stories

- They are attracted to successful people who can help them get even more results

- Good eye contact that speaks confidence

Identifying A Ruby In The Audience

- Get to the bottom line quickly

- Don't spend a lot of time chit-chatting

- Keep it short and results oriented

- Show them how they can hit their goals

- Show them their solutions to any of their problems

- Give them the ability to do it now – they hate to wait

- Challenge them to increase their lifestyle

- Make it all about them

Source: Taken from GEMS® Mastery Workbook by Dani Johnson

Based on what you have learned thus far about me and the descriptions of the GEMS®, can you tell which one or two are my dominant personality type/s? Well, I am 50/50 Sapphire and Ruby. Basically, I like to have fun (Sapphire), but when it comes to certain things, I don't play (Ruby). I draw the line when it comes to my health, faith, family, integrity, standing up for what's right and business. There's a time and a place for everything.

In Dani's GEMS® Mastery personality product, it's possible to have some aspects of each of the gem. I do have a tender heart, like a Pearl and organized like an Emerald. You will find that you also have elements of all of them, but the key is to associate with the dominant personality style. Just like the Generations, they are general descriptions based on majority.

When I first did the exercise, I was mostly Sapphire, about sixty percent, but that was because when I came into the room when Dani first started the exercise, all I heard was that the fun, energetic people needed to be on stage. Automatically, that was me. I love having fun and energy is like my middle name. This group were the Sapphires. As she started going through the descriptions of a Sapphire, I quickly realized that some of the styles were not me at all. I am not messy, unorganized or wear mis-matched clothing. This is quite the opposite. I am super organized, super clean and anal about stuff being around me and I must always match, always! I am a model and fashion diva and there's no way I am going out there looking like a clown. Well maybe not that colorful, but my shoes, clothes, accessories and all must match and make sense to me. I like to color coordinate so much, that I even make my children and spouse color co-ordinate with me.

Therefore, there may be elements of the personality descriptions that aren't you at all, but what you are looking for is if the majority describes you. It is a very effective tool that can be used to determine your personality style, because what I am attempting to narrow down is who are you? What's the authentic you? Without understanding you, it's impossible to lead others. It's actually impossible to lead yourself without knowing who you are, what are your traits, your skills, goals, personality type, generation, and such forth.

What would you consider to be your predominant GEM®?

Leadership Styles

In the previous sections, I shared a high-level overview of the different Generations and pointed out some of their strengths, weaknesses, opportunities for growth and potential threats for each generation. The new generation (Gen E) was introduced and are the Generation that starts now and how those of us that are alive and are leaders have an opportunity to mold Gen E into the generation that we would like them to be. There's also an opportunity for Generation Z (Centennials) to be molded into exceptional leaders. They are great listeners and are still in the age group where they are absorbing, molding, and experiencing. Centennials are also mostly the children of Generation X, as well the Millennials who are in the mid to late thirties to early forties and were raised with a different perspective than those born to Baby Boomers.

Most Gen-Xers were not mentored by the older generations and thus, they have developed a posture that they will give what they have not been given. It's similar to when someone was raised without a father or mother or perhaps very poor and have made it their life's mantra and mission that they will give what they have not been given. I see this in my husband, who grew up without his biological father and made a promise to himself at a very young age that if God blessed him to be a father that he would not leave his children, and he would be the best father to them as he knows how to be. He is indeed an excellent father and a great leader.

Just as there are generational differences, the same is true for leadership styles. Not all leaders lead the same way or even have the same viewpoint on leadership. Some leaders are more **transformational leaders, some situational, others transactional, functional, transitional**, a combination of both, neither or some other form of leadership style. Some leaders don't fit into any category and have created their own category. For the most part, however, leaders typically fall into one of the following categories above. Some people are dominantly one type of leadership style and others are several. The leadership styles are also based on the task, attitudes of the team or individuals, type of project, and more. The leadership style used when doing a task with elementary children on a project is different from that of doing a task with a community volunteer group or a business.

Transformational Leader

A transformational leader is one that looks at leadership from the perspective of change. They don't lead according to the status quo and are very solutions driven. Transformational leadership can be traced back to, J. M. Burns who first articulated the idea of transformational leadership in 1978 before Bernard Bass expanded on it almost a decade later (Lussier & Achua, 2013). As global challenges arise, there is a greater need for Leaders who can successfully craft and implement bold strategies that will transform or align their vision, the organization's vision with its strengths and weaknesses and be able to foresee emerging opportunities and threats. Increased volatility and uncertainty is seen as one of the contributing factors for the emergence of transformational leadership. Transformational leadership describes a process of positive influence that changes and transforms individuals, organizations, and communities (Lussier & Achua, 2013). There's a definite need for change.

No matter which area of influence I am involved in, transformational leadership is always at the core. It's wired in my DNA and it fits my personality and natural traits. Sometimes it has worked against me or not in my best interest, in organizations that aren't looking for change. They like things just the way they are and they like the good ole' days and the good ole' boys club and have no desire to change. Since I am a visionary, I am able to foresee what can be done differently to transform the organization. Not only do I know what can be done to make things better, but I also know the best approach to implement it. Organizations such as religious higher educational institutions, from my experience, are the ones that oftentimes are not receptive to transformational leadership. They seem to prefer situational leadership style.

A leader who employs the tactics of transformational leadership style is one who identifies what needs to be changed in a task or goal, how it should be done, and works towards the completed task. This style is used when the leadership desires to motivate and inspire the individual or team. It is based on self-motivation and structure. This type of leader has the ability to change the way one thinks and how they behave. The result is that they realize they have the ability to accomplish more than they realized in the beginning. This leadership style encourages others to ask questions and give examples or tell stories to clarify their points. This causes an "aha" moment or an awakening and that's one of the main goals of a transformational leader. (Vernonlex, 2015)

Situational Leadership

First introduced by Kenneth Blanchard and Paul Hersey, as leadership that is based on various situation. This is a case by case leadership style. It is more task driven, rather than overall leadership. Situational Leadership style best suit those who like to handle one thing at a time. Leaders in this role must adapt to the situation or the person and not the other way around. It has its place and serves well for many and is good for environments that are more technical in nature. When changes need to be made about technical systems or workflows, situational leaders work well in that setting. It's not necessary for a transformational leader to be heavily involved in technical system changes and the like, but it is for situational leaders.

Individuals that are selected to perform a task as a whole come with different personalities, experiences, abilities, and understanding. This is where situational leadership can be implemented to bring the group together and work towards a common goal successfully. A situational leader must be aware of the possible success or failure of a task based on the actions of the group. This means that a leader must be flexible in guiding the group and in how the task will be accomplished. It is important that the leader realizes that more than one leadership style can be implemented to keep the team on task and to reach the goal (Situational Leadership, 2018). This leadership style is effective in companies with multiple units, teams or divisions. Having a Situational Leader overseeing units or departments works very well. It's a win-win for leadership, because the Situational Leaders gets to exercise his or her strengths and the organization accomplishes its goals.

Transactional Leadership

Other forms of Leadership styles are Transactional and Functional leadership styles. Transactional leadership is more like management. They tend to like to manage and are aware of everything that's happening. They are perfect to lead human resources departments or organizations that heavily rely on personnel development as part of their structure. Transactional leaders like when things are under control and they typically don't like when things seem chaotic. It's sometimes difficult for them to see beyond the current circumstances at hand.

Transactional leadership is based on following a plan and inspiring others to work towards it. When a leader uses the transactional leadership style, the purpose is to guide a person or group with positive and negative reinforcement to motivate. The person or group will probably be new to group work or working on projects. The transactional leadership style is one where guidance, learning, and compliance are the tools used in order for the task or goal to be accomplished. The person or group is supervised every step of the way. The leader uses positive statements and consequences to motivate. This is accomplished by the leader implementing individual and group evaluations, instructions, task or goal criterion, and organization of the project. Everyone involved must abide by and know the chain of command (Everything You Need to Know About Transactional Leadership, 2018).

Functional Leadership

Functional Leadership is like team leadership. The functional leadership style is more of a behavior than a process. In fact, sometimes you will see the two types of leadership as one (functional and team). It focuses more on how leadership is being demonstrated rather than who's leading. Meaning that functional leaders just want to know that things are working and not who's working it. That's not important to them. Functional leadership works best in factory settings, behind the scenes production and hospitality working environments.

This type of leader must be active in evaluating the individual or group in order to accomplish a task or goal. This style looks for the leader to be aware of the needs of the individuals or group, so the task or goal can be met. The usefulness of the individual or group to do a task is the main concern. Areas of concern that a functional leader has are identifying the task and relaying that to the individual or group; making sure the group is functioning in a positive manner, and if not, what changes are necessary to make it so; and working with the individual or team in a positive way. (Shead, 2018)

Transitional Leadership

Finally, there are Transitional Leaders. When a business is downsizing, closing due to poor growth or sales, or getting ready to build in new locations, a Transitional Leadership style is usually brought in to facilitate the goal or task. The person who takes on the role of being a Transitional Leader is one that is recognized in a particular field locally, nationally, and globally for his or her abilities to get the job done.

Transitional leadership style focuses on management of an entity or individual. The transitional leadership style starts with leadership skills that are superior than the average person. This person must be an expert. What a Transitional Leader explores is how does the organization transition from one level to another. They evaluate if the change is necessary and why. They are able to develop a plan to accomplish that task or goal and implement a smooth transition from the present situation to an acceptable resolution regardless of the individual, company, business, or entity. Usually the kinds of persons that use transitional leadership skills are typically, retired board members or company presidents, consultants and mediators. When the transition is complete, that leader feels accomplished, because they successfully completed the task. (Ball, 2018)

While there are various leadership styles out there, for the most part, these are the more common leadership styles. These styles are not gender specific but are broader, describing more of how he or she tends to lead especially within an organization. Which style to employ can be based on the needs of the situation, the individual, team, or group they must work with and their knowledge and experience base. A leader knows when to combine two or more leadership styles to accomplish a task or goal. For instance, a Transitional Leader may also use situational and transactional leadership styles to motivate an individual or a team through the use of penalties or rewards.

Leadership styles vary, and none is better, per se than the other. It is all contingent on the environment and which style works best for that Leader. It is beneficial for those who do not know which leadership style works best for him or her to re-read this section and determine which Leadership Styles best describes him or her. Knowing your dominant leadership styles is imperative for the success of being a leader. It prevents conflicts, limits frustrations and time wasters and is a guide for determining what companies are a good fit for you and vice versa.

What would you consider to be your leadership style and why?

NOTES..........

Journal the Journey – Notes from this Chapter

CHAPTER 6

LAW #6: HOW HE LEADS

"The task of the leader is to get his people from where they are to where they have not been."

Henry Kissinger

There is no one universal definition for leadership or no one person can say this is the definition and no others matter, because that would not be true. Leadership is complex and is viewed differently in different cultures, class, environment and sectors. While there's no specific definition for leadership that is considered universal, I believe that there are general and universal differences between how men lead versus how women lead. Some of these differences are simply God-ordained, some are taught, some are based on experiences, culture, and such forth.

Men are wired differently from women and that's not something one can change. Women have a womb and men don't. Men have testicles and women don't, which means that their bodies go through changes that women don't experience and vice versa. Thus, for the very fact that a man's body is different from a woman, it goes without saying, that differences exist. Therefore, how a man leads, act and behaves is different from a woman and it should be. It would be alarming if it didn't.

Nevertheless, there are some differences that are taught either based on culture and/or being a product of an environment that affects one's viewpoint of leadership. How each of us were raised shapes our mindset, attitudes and leadership styles. For example, being raised Jamaican, I observed that little boys were told that crying is for girls. I would hear my family say to my brother "why do you cry so much, stop being a little girl." It probably wasn't said that nicely, but you get the jiff of what I'm saying. Little girls were taught that they are princesses and that they can cry all they want to, in fact, little girls got more attention when they cried.

This early on-set of behavioral differences and any learned behavior impacts who we become. For example, within a few years of my marriage, it dawned on me that I have never seen my husband cry. We endured some traumatic moments, that I cried about, but didn't see my husband cried. He wasn't a person that showed his emotions. He managed his emotions and it was more important for him to tend to my emotional needs than to his own. These differences led us to act differently and it caused some conflicts in our marriage. Through communication we were able to grow through them. Therefore, when we had children, we ensured that we allowed our son to be who he is, to cry if he's hurting and same thing for our girls. My husband and I wanted to ensure that we were not 'controlling' who they became, but rather allowing them to be who they were created to be as we guide, teach, coach and love them through their differences.

By nature, most women are typically more emotional than most men. Men have a tendency to lead more with their minds than with their hearts. Men most often times just want the facts so that they can get straight to the point. Women have a tendency of wanting to tell the whole story. They need to put their feelings and emotions into the story and sometimes will divert from the situation at hand. This is also the reason why women are great speakers and actresses as they tend to be able to get more in-depth into the story. A man's leadership style is usually direct, results driven, give me the bottom line, let's get it done, type of an attitude.

One of the reasons men are great leaders in Corporate America is because they are able to separate their home life from their professional life (not saying that's good). This is not to say that women cannot do the same, because they can, but it's easier for men to do it. Through my studies of differences between men and women, I've discovered that men are like boxes and women are like circles. Most men can only handle one thing at a time (one box at a time). If they are watching television, that's all they're doing and they're not cognizant of anything else that's going on around them. The house could be on fire, and they remain cool, calm and collective in that special box. Women on the other hand, tend to connect everything. Something that happened years ago, is somehow connected to something now and to her it's all related, but to the man, he doesn't understand what one thing has to do with another. This is actually a strength of a man as he's able to compartmentalize one issue versus another and this works well in certain settings.

Some weaknesses that affects how men lead are their lack of empathy. Since men tend to not be as visible with their emotions as women are, at times they may appear to not be caring and even come off as being cold. They may care and care quite a bit, but the inability to express it is oftentimes are viewed by women as being disconnected and coldhearted. However, male leaders who understands his or her purpose, is a visionary, shows empathy, and is confident in his abilities, is an **exceptional** leader. More importantly, if he has also experienced some hardships and challenges, that makes him even a greater leader. When a man who's an overcomer, has wisdom and understanding, that is also empathetic becomes a leader, that organization or home has a winner.

Therefore, in an effort to gather other perspectives on male leaders, and their thoughts on leadership, it was necessary to interview others to get their viewpoint on Leadership. All the leaders were asked the same questions as a means of integrity and validity. Allow the responses to shed some light on the fact that we all lead differently, and these differences can be strengths.

Meet Pastor Tafforest Brewer

TD Brewer, an influential public speaker, pastor, inventor, successful author and entrepreneur, who inspires people to transform their lives from within. He has been called an idea strategist, barrier breaker, life enthusiast, and master blessing teacher. His work has been responsible for transforming lives, creating personal and professional success stories, and for saving many from the pains and torments of depression and hopelessness.

He has a refreshing and liberating perspective and bases his teachings on the Hebrew writings of the Bible. His direct and compassionate approach generates strong responses from audiences across America.

He grew up poor and went on a journey of Bible research and self-discovery to overcome poverty. Because of his childhood experience, he is deeply passionate about equipping others with the tools necessary to live a healthy, happy, and prosperous life. He wants nothing more than to see others live a life of victory, and get the upper hand over life's circumstances, just like he did.

1. **Define Leadership in your own words**

   Leadership is the ability to discover greatness in others, therefore creating an environment to maximize their potential.

2. **What historical leadership act had the greatest impact on you and why?**

   Dr. Martin Luther King was a brilliant thinker that taught people how to be proud of who they were as a people and individual. His speeches challenged people to succeed and excel beyond the odds.

3. **What current act of leadership inspires you and why?**

   Accountability and integrity are real characteristics of a good leader. Leadership begins in the heart of an individual with a vision of empowering others. Jack Ma of Alibaba inspires me with his passion for improving the lives of others.

4. **What would you consider to be your leadership style?**

   I have a confident can-do style of leadership that makes room for individuals with different personalities to grow.

5. **What barrier, challenge, or test, did you face, that you overcame that has helped you to be the leader that you are today?**

I had to overcome the limited beliefs of others concerning my abilities. I had to learn to encourage myself daily, believe in myself daily, and educate myself daily.

Meet Dr. Anil Mehta

Dr. Anil Mehta, born in Mumbai, India in the year 1978, is a computer science researcher and entrepreneur. Since an early age Dr. Mehta has been involved in coding of computers. Being a son of Drs. Shillander Kumar Mehta and Rita S. Mehta, both respected scientists in their own right, and having siblings as researchers, entrepreneurs, doctors and high achievers, Dr. Mehta was immersed in an academic and thought-provoking environment from his childhood. This foundation led to many of his achievements later on in life including an PhD in Electrical and Computer engineering from Southern Illinois University Carbondale under the guidance of IEEE fellow Professor Viswanathan and deep collaborations with the world-famous Bell Laboratory and Mitsubishi electric research labs.

Dr. Mehta has published over 10 papers and 20 patents. Been part of half a dozen different start-ups and the formation of an institute of Innovation at Southern Illinois University, Carbondale.

Dr. Mehta now teaches Computer Science at Chicago State University and is the Founding Director of an Innovation laboratory at Chicago State University. He also is a radio station show host and CEO of Ka Wa Mamua, Inc., an history-based application located in Hawai'i.

1. **Define Leadership in your own words**

   "It is the art of seeing beyond the horizon into infinity and see things as the can be from as they are today, and to take the environment step-by-step towards that reality in a way that the people and environment naturally evolves into this reality."

2. **What historical leadership act or person had the greatest impact on you and why?**

   Back in 1995 in India, new colleges were being build which created new opportunities for students to attend school. In order to get into the college, a seat had to be available, otherwise you could not attend. It was like getting a seat on an airplane. There was one centralized admissions office regardless of which college the students wanted to attend. My parents and I applied for a seat at one of the colleges, but unfortunately it was told to us that the seats were filled and that when others became available that I would get in.

When the seats did become available the admissions department decided to not offer those seats. There was confusion about how the seats were being allocated and myself along with several other students were told that we needed to re-apply in order to get a seat. This became an issue so Dr. Shillander Kumar Mehta, a renewed scientist, my father and a few others, insisted that those seats be made available so that I could go to college, as well as others. He pursued and did not quit until we were able to go to college. From this selfless act of leadership, today I am an engineer and a PhD Graduate had it not been for my father and the other parents that fought. It not only benefited me, but countless others as well, who today would probably not be where they are or who they are, had it not been for leaders who (**act**) on their leadership.

3. What current act of leadership inspires you and why?

Makerspaces and innovation is what inspires me. Those that created Makerspaces are genius'. It is an act of sharing and making everyone feel involved. I like a sense of community with makerspaces.

4. What would you consider to be your leadership style?

Social-collective...I think bringing everyone together on the same page is a great start to leadership.

5. **What barrier, challenge, or test, did you face, that you overcame that has helped you to be the leader that you are today?**

The ability to believe in myself, knowing that all will be well.

Meet Mayor Ken Baer

Mayor Ken Baer is married to Judy Baer for 50 years and together they have three children and 10 grandchildren. He has a Bachelor of Science Degree in civil engineering and a Master of Science Degree in Professional Management. He's a retired U.S. Navy officer, rank of Commander and is the Mayor of Perryville, Missouri and a part time cattle rancher.

1. **Define Leadership in your own words**

   Develop your vision

   - Develop your plan to accomplish the vision

   - Build your team to implement the plan

   - Motivate your team through communication and trust

2. **What historical leadership act had the greatest impact on you and why?**

   Winston Churchill ------ Take risks and never give up

   Ronald Reagan ------ The Great Communicator

156

3. **What current act of leadership inspires you and why?**

Donald Trump --------- Disrupt the status quo, take risks, negotiate, communicate directly.

4. **What would you consider to be your leadership style?**

Persuasion to get your team to align with you, develop trust, know the issues and study the issues. Complete integrity and selflessness.

5. **What barrier, challenge, or test, did you face, that you overcame that has helped you to be the leader that you are today?**

Preconceived notion of what is true. A complete paradigm shift is sometimes necessary for the leader as well as for the team. This will take time and open mindedness.

Meet Minister Stephen Bent

Stephen Bent is a native of Milwaukee, Wisconsin and has lived in Springfield, Missouri since 2000. Since 2013, Stephen has been involved with Leadership Team Development. Inc. and is responsible for helping develop and build teams of business owners and entrepreneurs to help them pursue their dreams and goals. Since 2017, Stephen has also become partner with Buddy Webb & Company Architects. Stephen received his Bachelor of

Architecture at Drury University in Springfield, Missouri. Stephen currently resides in Springfield, Missouri with his wife and three children.

1. Define Leadership in your own words

Leadership is the ability to inspire vision, motivate and inspire individuals to engage and pursue their dreams and goals all comprised with integrity.

2. What historical leadership act had the greatest impact on you and why?

Martin Luther King. In the face of adversity and challenges, he remained a leader with integrity and standards that helped cultivate the freedoms that we share today. His stance on equality and love is a driving factor for me.

3. What current act of leadership inspires you and why?

A current act of leadership and example is from my mentor. He has been a rock and a true example of leadership and living without excuses. His leadership and example, along with my faith, are what I use as a compass to help guide my life.

4. What would you consider to be your leadership style?

I would consider my leadership style to be relaxed confidence mixed with compassion yet boldness. A leader has to lead regardless of his or her feelings. I've been taught that you feel the emotion but do the right thing anyway. I've been taught the acronym "F.I.O.": Figure It Out and I have definitely learned this through my mentor and his leadership and it has been incorporated into my leadership style. I have also learned how to be flexible but still hold high my standards and level of excellence.

5. What barrier, challenge, or test, did you face, that you overcame that has helped you to be the leader that you are today?

There were two events in my life that has developed me into the person I am today. Those were the passing of my late wife, Sherri, in 2012 and the passing of my mother, Sandra, in 2016. With the passing of Sherri, I was instantly left as a single dad raising two small children by myself, which was quite a challenge. These two events really opened my eyes to who I really was. Challenges and adversity do not make the man, they reveal the man and who you really are. It was revealed to me how strong I really am, and strength is a characteristic of any leader that has gone through challenges and has overcome.

From the responses from these male leaders, it's evident that who one becomes is shaped from different experiences, situations and acts. Different experiences in one's life shape's how he or she leads and the path in which one takes. Dr. Mehta for example, his path was shaped based on his father's ability to fight for him to receive an education. He's quite fortunate to have parents, especially a father to fight on his behalf. One of the reasons why I am writing this book is for this book to be the father, the mother, mentor, that go to guide, that resource that fights for you. Use the principles, concepts, stories and examples in the **10 Laws of Leadership** to lead your ship.

 ## ACTION STEPS!

TO DO!

If you're a male, please answer the following:

1) Define Leadership in your own words

2) What historical leadership act or person has had the greatest impact on you and why?

3) What current act of leadership inspires you and why?

4) What would you consider to be your leadership style?

5) What barrier, challenge, or test, did you face, that you overcame that has helped you to be the leader that you are today?

Leadership is about Endurance

Meet Dr. Bill Winston

Dr. William Samuel Winston (aka Bill Winston) born in Tuskegee, Alabama, was inspired and influenced for leadership by the numerous educators, scientists, and physicians who surrounded him as a youth, and by the historic aviation accomplishments of the Tuskegee Airmen who served as his role models. He is a graduate of the internationally known Tuskegee Institute (now Tuskegee University), in Tuskegee, Alabama, where Booker T. Washington's and George Washington Carver's legacies of leadership and invention permeated the environment. He is known as an American preacher, author, visionary, leader and business entrepreneur. Dr. Winston served for six years as a fighter pilot in the United States Air Force, where his extraordinary achievements in aerial flight earned him The Distinguished Flying Cross, The Air Medal for performance in combat, and the Squadron Top Gun Award.

He is the founder and senior pastor of Living Word Christian Center (LWCC), a multi-cultural, non-denominational church with more than 20,000 members located in Forest Park, Illinois, and Living Word Christian Center-Tuskegee, in Tuskegee, Alabama. LWCC has a broad range of ministries and related entities. Dr. Winston is also the founder and president of the nationally accredited Joseph Business School (JBS), which teaches practical and biblical principles to empower adults to develop indispensable skills as successful entrepreneurs and business leaders. JBS is located in Forest Park, Illinois with partnership locations on five continents. The Joseph Business School also has an online program.

He is also the founder of Bill Winston Ministries (BWM), a partnership-based global outreach ministry. BWM produces the Believer's Walk of Faith television and radio program reaching over 800 million households worldwide.

Dr. Winston also has 882 national and international churches and ministries under his spiritual covering through Faith Ministries Alliance (FMA). His ministry owns and operates two shopping malls, Forest Park Plaza, in Forest Park, IL, and Washington Plaza in Tuskegee. He is also the founder and CEO of Golden Eagle Aviation, a fixed base operation (FBO) located at the historic Moton Field in Tuskegee.

Sources: https://www.billwinston.org/bwinston/ and https://believersportal.com/biography-dr-bill-winston/

Dr. Winston is unstoppable. If you ever desire to see leadership in action, then visit the campus in Forest Park, IL. My family and I have been privileged to be VIP whenever we visit his ministry. We've gotten a tour of the campus on golf carts and it's an amazing site to experience. We learned that he had to endure several no's and scrutiny from those who tried to hinder his progress. Through it all, Dr. Winston continues to win, because he has endurance.

Leadership is about Integrity

Meet Evangelist Billy Graham (1918-2018)

Born on November 7, 1918, in Charlotte, North Carolina. His early beginnings started when he had an opportunity to preach at a revival in Los Angeles and then as a guest on Stuart Hamblen's radio show in 1949. The publicity made Graham a superstar and he began broadcasting his sermons globally. Though detractors criticized Graham for being too liberal, one Time reporter dubbed him "the Pope of Protestant America." Graham retired in 2005, and later died at his North Carolina home on February 21, 2018, at the age 99. In hindsight there was little indication that Graham would one day preach the Christian gospel to as many as 215 million people and live audiences over 185 countries. Graham has been credited with preaching to more individuals than anyone else in history, not counting the additional millions he has addressed through radio, television and the written word. Thus, Graham helped bind together a vulnerable nation through religious revival. By glazing over the finer details of Christianity and focusing on more moderate doctrines, Graham made evangelism enticing, non-threatening, even easy—and the media made his messages accessible to the masses.

Life Timeline:

- 1934 – Committed his life to Jesus Christ

- 1947-1952 – President of Northwestern Schools

- 1949 – Gained national attention with Los Angeles crusade

Challenges:

- Graham's detractors have criticized him for being too liberal and refusing to play into partisan politics.

- President Truman even went so far as to call Graham a "counterfeit."

- Some anti-Semitic comments between Graham and President Nixon were also caught on tape in 1972.

Wins:

- 1950 – Founded Billy Graham Evangelistic Association

- 1956 – Founded Christianity Today Magazine

- 1957 – Led a New York City crusade in Madison Square Garden nightly for 16 weeks

- 1966 – Convened the World Congress on Evangelism in Berlin

- 1982 – Awarded Templeton Foundation Prize for Progress in Religion

- 2007 – Billy Graham Library in Charlotte, NC opened

- Graham was awarded the Ronald Reagan Presidential Foundation Freedom Award, the Congressional Gold Medal, the Templeton Foundation Prize for Progress in Religion, the Big Brother Award, the Templeton Prize for Progress in Religion, and the Speaker of the Year Award. Additionally, Graham was recognized by the National Conference of Christians and Jews for promoting understanding between faiths and bestowed with the Honorary Knight Commander of the Order of the British Empire (KBE).

Source: https://www.christianheadlines.com/blog/a-timeline-of-the-life-of-billy-graham.html and
https://www.biography.com/people/billy-graham-9317669

Mr. Graham was a man that led with integrity. No matter how much he was criticized, he continued ministering the word of God and his following grew. He was a man of principle and lived his life purposefully. Leadership is about never wavering but standing on one's values and beliefs and that's what Billy Graham did.

Leadership is about Social Responsibility

Meet Mark Zuckerberg

Mark Zuckerberg from White Plains, New York, born May 14, 1984, is co-founder and CEO of the social-networking website Facebook, which has made him be known as one of the world's youngest billionaires. He co-founded the social-networking platform, Facebook out of his college dorm room. He left Harvard after his sophomore year to concentrate on the site. Since inception, Facebook has grown to more than 2 billion people.

The birth of Facebook was portrayed in the 2010 film *The Social Network*. In it he created a messaging program named "Zucknet" and Mark Zuckerberg stated, "I had a bunch of friends who were artists," he said. "They'd come over, draw stuff, and I'd build a game out of it." Since amassing his sizeable fortune, Zuckerberg has used his millions to fund a variety of philanthropic causes. The most notable examples came in 2010 when he donated $100 million to save the failing Newark Public Schools system in New Jersey. Then, in December 2010, Zuckerberg signed the "Giving Pledge", promising to donate at least 50 percent of his wealth to charity over the course of his lifetime. Other Giving Pledge members includes Bill Gates, Warren Buffett and George Lucas. After his donation, Zuckerberg called on other young, wealthy entrepreneurs to follow suit. "With a generation of younger folks who have thrived on the success of their companies, there is a big opportunity for many of us to give back earlier in our lifetime and see the impact of our philanthropic efforts," he said

Challenges:

- 2009 book *The Accidental Billionaires,* by writer Ben Mezrich, hit stores, which told the store of Zuckerberg's life, which Mezrich sold the rights, resulting in the film The Social Network. Zuckerberg claims many of the tales within the movie were inaccurate.

Struggles:

- In 2006, the business mogul faced his first big hurdle. The creators of Harvard Connection claimed that Zuckerberg stole their idea and insisted the software developer needed to pay for their business losses. Instant Messages revealed Zuckerberg may have intentionally stolen the intellectual property of Harvard Connection and Offered Facebook user's private information to his friends.

- After enduring criticism for the proliferation of fake news posts on his site leading up to the 2016 U.S. presidential election, Zuckerberg in early 2018 announced his personal challenge to develop improved methods for defending Facebook users from abuse and interference by nation-states.

- Zuckerberg came under fire again a few months later when it was revealed that Cambridge Analytica, a data firm with ties to President Donald Trump's 2016 campaign, had used private information from approximately 87 million Facebook profiles without the social network alerting its owners. The resulting outcry seemed to shake investors' confidence in Facebook, its shares dropping by 15 percent after the news became public.

- Testifies before the Senate Commerce and Judiciary Committees

Wins:

- Facebook had its initial public offering, raising $16 billion, making it the largest internet IPO in history

- September 2016, Zuckerberg and Chan announced that the Chan Zuckerberg Initiative (CZI), the company into which they put their Facebook shares, would invest at least $3 billion into scientific research over the next decade to help "cure, prevent and manage all diseases in our children's lifetime."

Mark's story is yet another leader that shows that being in leadership roles will at times be a struggle. There will be times when others on the team make a mistake or do something without you knowing and in the end it's always the responsibility of the leader to take responsibility. Mark has done just that. Though Facebook's platform is very innovative, and it will only continue to get better, it also comes with its share of problems. I admire how he's socially responsible and takes ownership for his company's mis-haps.

NOTES..........

Journal the Journey – Notes from this Chapter

NOTES...........

Journal the Journey – Notes from this Chapter

CHAPTER 7

LAW #7: HOW SHE LEADS

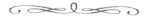

"Leadership is not about a popularity contest; it's about leaving your ego at the door. The name of the game is to lead without a title."

Robin S. Sharma

It's a gut feeling! I can feel it! Something isn't right! These are just some of the expressions that I have heard countless women express, including my mom, aunts and myself. These expressions of internal inclinations have prevented major disasters, deadly decisions, and unfortunate situations. These expressions have also been referred to as 'a six sense.' Women are such great leaders and decision makers, because they have an innate gut feeling that was given to them by God and wired in their womb, that men do not have. My husband is very aware of this, because he typically does not like to make a decision without running it by me. Women may not have all the answers, or the entire picture, but the answers that they do have are normally right. When a woman isn't sure about something, because of that gut feeling which she most often times go with, it would behoove her followers to listen to what she's feeling and saying.

"Women may not have all the answers, but the ones she does have, are normally right"

Tweet

Dr. Carolyn

As mentioned in the previous chapter, most women are more emotional than men as designed by God. I mentioned that this can sometimes delay a decision-making process in certain settings. However, being an emotional, deeply connected and wired being is also a strength in other settings. Shortly after losing twin boys at five (5) months gestation age, which was a major traumatic moment for my husband and I, followed by a miscarriage, I remember saying to myself that something isn't right. Emotionally I was distraught, and it was that same feeling that led to begin to research, ask questions and determine the problem and the solution. My husband took what was happening as face value, meaning that he just thought it was just something that happens in people's lives. To me what was natural is to have children, not to lose them.

Based on being an emotional being and not settling for the status quo, I made some changes, worked with a different physician, listened to and followed that gut feeling and today, we are the happy parents of three (3) adorable children. When it comes to being leaders of one's well-being, whether personally and professionally, emotions are a strength. A woman's love and care run deep and while she can quickly make a decision on matters in corporate settings, if she needs time to make that decision, it's normally for a good reason. The leadership skills and traits of a run are exhibited on land, sea or air.

On Tuesday, April 17, 2018, Southwest Airlines flight 1380 departing from New York City to Dallas experienced a mid-air engine explosion that turned into a life or death situation. One of the skills of a great leader is to remain focused in the midst of chaos. This is the case with Southwest Captain Tammie Jo Shults as she learned about the emergency on board and prepare for landing at Philadelphia International Airport. Captain Shults calmly described conditions on the craft to the air traffic controller: "Southwest 1380, we're single engine," said Shults, a former fighter pilot with the U.S. Navy. "We have part of the aircraft missing, so we're going to need to slow down a bit." She asked for medical personnel to meet the aircraft on the runway. "We've got injured passengers." "Injured passengers, okay, and is your airplane physically on fire?" asked the air traffic controller. "No, it's not on fire, but part of its missing," Shults said, pausing for a moment. "They said there's a hole, and, uh, someone went out." Her heroic leadership skills of being calm in the midst of chaos save 148 lives. There were 144 passengers on the flight and five (5) crew members, but unfortunately, one passenger passed away due the trauma she suffered when the window was shattered from debris from the engine that exploded. Her emotional state was to remain calm in the midst of chaos and her leadership skills saved lives.

Source: https://www.nytimes.com/2018/04/18/us/southwest-plane-engine-failure.html

Today when people think about leadership, images come to mind of powerful dynamic individuals who command victorious armies, shape the events of nations, develop religions, or direct corporate empires (Lussier & Achua, 2013). Leadership however, is not always the mainstream visible leaders that are observed and seen every day, but also those whom I refer to as the "hidden heroes." They are the ones that no one knows but a small group of people, sometimes just those at home.

Some of the greatest leaders not known to many are those that have serve their families and served them well. The bible states that "For if a man knows not how to rule his own house, how shall he take care of the church of God?" (1 Tim 3:5 KJV), thus leadership begins at home. One must first know how to govern and lead oneself at home without first attempting to lead outside of the house. The home is the training ground for professional leadership. If the children in the home don't listen to you, chances are, the folks out there will also not listen. If leadership was being practiced daily at home, I believe that here would not be so many problems in organizations. If the outside and the inside leader is the same person, whose desire is to serve first whether it's at home or work, then lead, the world would be a better place to live and work. Leadership would not have gotten so off track, so lost, and so distorted. Authentic leadership is the art of leading even when you don't feel like a leader or get recognized for your leadership.

Meet Sharon Spence

Sharon Rhonica Spence, born March 28, 1955 in the beautiful island of Jamaica. Sharon migrated to England at the age of 10 after her father (a West Indian) passed away, leaving her Mother with eight kids to raise. Coming back to the island shortly after graduating from high school, Sharon met Lynval Alascels Spence, the two fell in love and started a beautiful union. They have been married for 43 years, with three (3) wonderful children. Sharon spent her early days as a Nursing Assistant and most of her career as an Executive Mom and Entrepreneur, running the affairs of the family's transportation business, caring for her children and building a legacy that goes without saying. Sharon Spence is a legend, she's a visionary, she's a kind-hearted woman, she's unstoppable, she's my mom.

1. **Define Leadership in your own words**

Leadership is about being the best you. It's about loving and caring for others.

2. **What historical leadership act or person has had the greatest impact on you and why?**

My late Mother, Lucille Virgo-Hume. She was the epiphany of leadership. I saw my mom struggling through hardship when my father died, leaving her with nine children to raise on her won. She raised us the best way she could, and she did so without complaining. We were always fed, clothe and didn't feel like we were without, perhaps because of her strong faith in God. She was a giving woman and that inspired me to always be a giver. I find great joy to give.

3. What current act of leadership inspires you and why?

The current act of leadership that inspires me, is the unstoppable spirit of my daughter Carolyn. I knew from birth that she was someone special, I just didn't know that she would accomplish so much in such a short timeframe. She stops at nothing, going after everything she desires. She's also very giving and kind, and that inspires me to keep giving. She's a great mom and wife and is the rising star of today. I actually don't know how she does it, finding time for everything in her life and being successful at them all. This book alone that she's writing is an inspiration to me and says a lot about the great leader that my daughter (Dr. Carolyn G. Anderson is.

4. What would you consider to be your leadership style?

I would consider my leadership style to be more situational and peaceful. I like when everyone gets along in my family and workplace. I'll do my best to resolve conflicts and will always be the first one to make amends. I believe that communication is the key to leading effectively.

5. **What barrier, challenge, or test, did you face, that you overcame that has helped you to be the leader that you are today?**

Hmmm, let's see which ones. I've had many challenges and tests. From being in deadly car crashes, to having to leave my country to find work, to moments of not being able to afford paying for my home and so much more. I've hit some lows and have had some down moments, but through it all, I have learned that faith is what I need to get me through all of life's circumstances and that's what has made me the leader that I am today.

Meet Dr. Donna Cook

Dr. Donna Lynn Cook, born in Hattiesburg, MS, grew up in Flint, Michigan and now a resident of San Diego California. She has a Bachelor of Science in Nursing from the University of Southern Mississippi, Hattiesburg, MS, a Master of Science in Nursing - Wayne State University, Detroit, MI and a Doctor of Philosophy in Nursing - University of San Diego, San Diego, CA

Dr. Cook is a Certified Psychiatric Clinical Nurse Specialist at the San Diego Veterans Health Care System. She is also in private practice with Omni Behavioral Health, which she founded in 2013. Her research interest includes factors impacting people of color, especially African-American women. She is a proud member of Alpha Kappa Alpha Sorority, Inc.

1) Define Leadership in your own words

First and foremost, leadership is about creating a vision and then motivating, encouraging, supporting, guiding and inspiring others to fully engage and share in the implementation of that vision.

2) What historical leadership act or person has had the greatest impact on you and why?

The Civil Rights Movement was the most powerful manifestation of organized leadership in the world!! It was the result of the vision of a few, who collaborated, strategized and empowered the marginalized, who had no voice, to rise up and be heard. The results of that movement still inform the sociopolitical status of our nation and the world today.

3) What current act of leadership inspires you and why?

I am very inspired by the leadership style of the International President of Alpha Kappa Alpha Sorority, Incorporated, Dr. Dorothy Buckhanan Wilson, who has successfully lead the organization with brilliance, grace, humility and compassion. Dr. Buckhanan created a vision in total alignment with the motto of the organization, which is "Service to All Mankind" and has motivated and inspired members of AKA to implement her vision on an international level, resulting in a positive global impact.

4) What would you consider to be your leadership style?

I am a SERVANT-LEADER with a natural heart of giving, spiritually grounded in compassion, with an eternal vision of improving and enriching the lives of individuals and empowering organizations to improve the human condition locally, nationally and globally.

5) What barrier, challenge, or test, did you face, that you overcame that has helped you to be the leader that you are today?

I am tremendously inspired by The Four Agreements written by Don Miguel Ruiz, especially in dealing with the challenges involving interpersonal conflict. Simply stated, it is imperative to "be impeccable with my word" which I see as essential to having the trust and respect of others; "don't take anything personally" because it's not about ME, it's about collaborating with others to implement the vision; "don't make assumptions "regarding the thoughts, intentions or motivations of others. Don't write the story in your own head!! ASK Questions!! Open communication is the key element!!!! And lastly, "always do my best" assertively giving myself a voice, while fully respecting and giving voice to others. When I follow these principles, there is almost always a positive, productive and profound outcome!!

Meet Attorney Sheila Parrish-Spence

Atty. Sheila Parrish was born in Brooklyn, New York. She is the mother of Jonathan Spence, and a cute chihuahua – Prince. She presently lives in Milwaukee, Wisconsin. She received a Juris Doctorate in Law (JD) from North Carolina Central University Law School and was published in the schools Law Journal on "Due Process and Juvenile Protection. She's currently a sole proprietor at Sheila Parrish-Spence's Law Office. Her accomplishments are many, including being a part of professional organizations, such as; State Bar of Wisconsin, Inns of Court – Leander Foley Section, Phi Alpha Delta Legal Fraternity – co-founder Raymond Watkins Chapter, Alpha Phi Sigma – National Criminal Justice Honor Society.

1. Define Leadership in your own words

Leadership is the ability to guide and influence others on many levels with a successful outcome.

2. What historical leadership act or person has had the greatest impact on you and why?

Historically, the one person that had the greatest impact on me and shaping me as a leader was my father, the late Honorable Milwaukee County Circuit Court Judge Clarence R. Parrish. He taught me that attitude and communication are everything for success for myself, and for others. He had many teaching moments that were examples of leadership and success. I have and will continue to implement them throughout my life.

3. What current act of leadership inspires you and why?

I tend to be one who observes people, places, and things. As a result, I am exposed to various acts of leadership which inspire me. Some of the acts of leadership I tend to observe are in various fields of family relations, the legal field, education, social work, and religion. Each person in these fields have their own leadership styles – no two are alike. The bottom line is whether the task or goal is successful.

4. What would you consider to be your leadership style?

My leadership style is transitional. I am a fixer. When a person or organization is in need of change and needs an expert in the field who is not a friend or part of the organization, I am called in to access the situation, given recommendations, and if they are accepted, work towards specific goals. When my task is completed, I am finished and go on to my next project.

5. **What barrier, challenge, or test, did you face, that you overcame that has helped you to be the leader that you are today?**

Many people that are leaders have barriers, challenges, or tests in their lives that they attribute to their success in being a leader. The interesting thing is that most leaders did not set out to be a leader. They just aimed at being good at whatever they did. That is how I feel about myself. I have traveled throughout the world, met many people, experienced various cultures, and learned from each experience. Throughout my life I have enjoyed being a lawyer, mediator, adjunct professor, published author, started several small businesses, served on many boards, held many administrative positions, and more. All of these had their own barriers, challenges, or test be they communicating with others who did not want to participate, listening to others with understanding, knowing and implementing the rules, staying ethically straight in manner and purpose, and having the ability to be a critical thinker. All of these helped me be the leader I am today.

ACTION STEPS!

If you're a female, please answer the following:

1. Define Leadership in your own words

2. What historical leadership act or person has had the greatest impact on you and why?

3. What current act of leadership inspires you and why?

4. What would you consider to be your leadership style?

5. What barrier, challenge, or test, did you face, that you overcame that has helped you to be the leader that you are today?

These impactful responses of the leaders validate that women have the qualities that are needed to be successful leaders. The women leaders of today range from executives of the home to executives of in the boardroom. Whether they are taking care of children, or running a Fortune 500 Company, what is clear is that they have the guts and stamina to persevere through life's challenges and win. They are strong women with tenacity, drive, education, thoughtfulness, vulnerability, kindhearted, respect and are excellent decision makers. They know when to use what skill that is necessary for the task or work at hand. Leadership is not about backing down or giving up, but about growing through the pain which births forth purpose. It's about being confident in knowing who you are and what you were born to be and to do.

There are many mainstream leaders today, who had to go through trials and tribulations to get where they are today. Sometimes society will gloat on the fame, not realizing that there's a story behind the glory. Meet these leaders who are demonstrating that there's a leader in each of us and it takes excellence, persistence, drive, influence, motivation and other characteristics to be and remain a leader. It is possible and doable.

Leadership is about Perseverance

Meet Hillary Rodham Clinton

Hillary Clinton was born in Chicago, IL in 1947. She graduated from Wellesley College in 1969 and later attended Yale Law, where she met former president Bill Clinton. She advised on the Watergate investigation. When Bill became President, she advocated for the Health Care Act reform. She was the first former First Lady to hold a seat in the U.S. Secretary position. During her term as S.O.S., she took many initiatives, such as; human rights, woman's rights, and connected the US diplomatic efforts in Arab Spring intervention in Libya. She then decided to run for President in 2016 and won the bid as the Democratic Party representative.

She faced many trials and tribulations dealing with security breaches and issues dealing with Bill's past of infidelity and scandal. Although she faced many trials to make her seem unfit to become president of the United States, she became the first woman to campaign in the presidency. She made sure to include that everyone had to be involved, and it did not just take one person to run the country. Since her campaign loss, she has started charities, written books about the loss of losing the presidential election and has not given up on helping our country. She started out as a law student, took an active role as First Lady, was successful as a U.S. Secretary of State, a win as the Democratic Presidential Nominee, and now, living life fully every day, after politics.

Source: Hillary Clinton: (https://www.biography.com/people/hillary-clinton-9251306)

Lessons learned about Leadership

Hillary teaches me that when you are a leader, it doesn't mean that you will not have your share of troubles. You will, but it is how one responds to the tough situations that determines the level of success that he or she reaches. Hillary faced many ups and downs in her life, but she didn't quit. She's an example of leadership in action. After her presidential defeat in 2016 to President Donald Trump, she showed up at one of the events at the Inauguration Ceremony, perhaps with despair and pain, yet her very presence spoke volume without giving much explanation. She demonstrated respect and honor. She showed what it's like to persevere even when the natural body doesn't want to. She was more than likely sitting in the midst of those who probably didn't vote for her and the person that was her opponent, yet she persevered. Without words that's leadership.

Leadership is about Influence

Meet Oprah Winfrey

Oprah Winfrey was born in 1954 in Mississippi. In 1974, she moved to Baltimore where she hosted a talk show. After hosting different shows and being a news anchor, she then caught her big break and hosted her own show from 1986 to 2011 in Chicago, IL. Shortly after her daytime talk show ended, she launched her own television network – The Oprah Winfrey Network (OWN).

According to Forbes Magazine, she was one of the wealthiest African American women in the 20th century and the world's only black billionaire for three years straight. Her Angel network has raised over 50 million dollars for various charitable programs. In 1994 she then proposed a bill that would later be passed into law, that would establish a database of convicted child abusers. In November 2013, she received the nation's highest civilian honor from former President Obama, The Presidential Medal of Freedom. He gave her this honor for her contributions to the country.

Coming from a childhood of abuse, sometimes ridiculed in the entertainment industry, especially through comedy, yet she doesn't stop. She has become one of the most respected women of our time and rightfully so.

Source: Oprah Winfrey:

(https://www.biography.com/people/oprah-winfrey-9534419)

Lessons learned about Leadership

There are so many lessons that can be learned from Oprah's story. Even though most of what we see is through television, it feels like she's a family member living in our home. She has been open with her struggles, ups and downs and has taken us on her life's journey. Oprah tenacity, transparency and principles are transparent and are excellent characteristics of leadership. Oprah is determined to win and that she does. She's a trendsetter, a trailblazer and one that uses her influence to lead.

Leadership is about Transparency

Meet Dani Johnson

Dani Johnson has led hundreds of thousands of people throughout the world with her expert teachings on business, money and relationships, all while teaching about enjoying life. She was once living out of her car and had $2.03 to her name. She then turned it around by the age of 23 and became a millionaire. With her drive and persistence, she built her business from the ground up, literally. She is now an advocate for helping other people start their businesses from whatever stage they are in. She has built homes for the extremely poor world-wide, fed and clothed the homeless, and rescued children from the sex trade and educated them.

Source: Dani Johnson (www.danijohnson.com/about)

From being in Dani's presence physically and being an insider with danijohnson.com, I've had the opportunity to first hand learn from her. She shares her story all the time about her struggles, fears, losses, brokenness and her traumatic childhood. She reminds me of me and that's perhaps why I like her so much, because one of the strengths of a great leader is transparency. Telling one's story helps others to overcome and hang on when things get difficult. Leaders that hide their story or sugar coat their history oftentimes do not connect well with others because the authenticity is missing. Dani story for leaders is that going through tough times is only a set-up for success. It's like the law of reciprocity. Give and you shall receive, if you've been low then you shall go high. Sow and you shall reap.

Whether you are just starting your leadership journey or very seasoned, know that the tough moments that you have experienced or is experiencing is a part of your journey. It's something that your followers will admire and probably relate to. Therefore, don't attempt to skip-out on that process, otherwise you may be hindering the authenticity of your story and most people do not want to listen to someone who has never been through something. Personally, I like to hear, what you've been through, how did you come through so that I at least have a guide for when I'm going through.

NOTES..........

Journal the Journey – Notes from this Chapter

NOTES..........

Journal the Journey – Notes from this Chapter

CHAPTER 8

LAW #8: HOW THEY LEAD

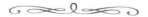

"The secret to success is good leadership, and good leadership is all about making the lives of the team members or workers better."

Tony Dungy

Like a beautiful sunrise and the calm sweetness of a sunset, so is the sight of a man and woman working together towards one common goal. The cohesiveness of putting the strengths of a man and the wisdom of a woman together produces exceptional results.

It's even more magnificent when it is a husband and wife team working whether in business or in the home. One of the laws of leadership is learning how to work together and putting aside gender differences, considering that the gender differences are actually complimentary to each other. God knew what He was doing when He made males the way they are, and females the way they are. They were designed to be different. They were created to think differently, to see things differently and to use those differences as strengths. Remember that gut feeling that I mentioned before that most women embody? Imagine putting that gut feeling with the mindset of a purpose-driven male and the two pursue together. They become an unstoppable force to be reckon with whether working in a personal or professional setting. I have experienced this over and over again.

Once upon a time when I was the Manager at an Insurance Company, reporting always to male Directors which I absolutely loved, none of them made leadership decisions unless I was involved. They relied on my intuition, leadership and wisdom to make concrete decisions. Our department was responsible for all the Physician and Hospital contracts and we were successful in working together to make things happen. It was such a fun relationship and I didn't know any other way to be.

Only once in my professional career did I report to a female and I didn't like it (lol). She was a micro manager and it was more about her feelings that the work that needed to be done for the company.

She had an issue about everything and would walk around the office just watching everyone. It was probably just her and not necessarily because she was a female, because no one liked her. Nevertheless, it was the only experience I have that I can share. I believe this helped to shape how I led, because I wanted to make sure that I didn't do what she did. Leadership should be fun and enjoyable. The team should enjoy working with you and for you. Leadership is about allowing others to be themselves and to learn from their mistakes. Leadership is about leading authentically, living purposefully, amidst chaos at home, work or play.

"Leadership is like a baseball game. You start and win at home-base"

Tweet

Dr. Carolyn

Leadership begins at home. In order to be an effective leader outside of the home, first that leader must be effective at home. Leadership is like a baseball game, you start at home base and win at home base. If the player is stuck out on second base, and never make it back around to home base, there's no score given. The same is true for leadership. I've seen so many leaders, who cannot lead his or her team at home and attempt to be an effective leader professionally. They go back and forth from home-base to 1st base, never quite making it to 2nd and 3rd base successful, so that he or she can win. This becomes a daily pattern – hit the ball-run to 1st base, with no one else on the team that can hit the ball so that you can run to the next bases. This is because everyone on the team is doing the same thing; unsuccessful at home and attempting to lead in the workplace. This applies to single or married couples.

A single person must know how to effectively use his or her time. They must know how to prepare healthy meals and take care of his or her wellbeing. A single person must lead his or her finances and not overspend or over indulge because he or she is single. As a matter of fact, adding children, spouses and/or parents to the equation actually makes leadership at home more difficult. Thus, whether the person is single, married, with or without children, leadership must exist and start at home first. Leaders lead by example, even when no human being is looking. There is always someone watching! God!

My husband and I have been working together pretty much since we were engaged. We planned our wedding together, literally. Typically, you will find that the female is the one that does most of the wedding plans. This wasn't the case for Kevel and me. He was very involved in all the planning and preparation leading up to the day of the wedding. In actuality, he may have done just a little bit more than me, (maybe, just a little....lol).

Our working together continued after we got married. He was the youth director of a program at our local church and I was his assistant, filling in where he needed me to. We knew our roles and we were well prepared each time we had the youth meetings. There was no confusion about who does what and if either of us neither to step in and fill each other's role, we knew what to do. I knew that he was the director and I was more like the manager, but he never let me feel as if I was less than he was or that he was supreme over me. In fact, it was quite the opposite. He relied heavily on the skillset that I had to accomplish whatever task that was needed. I also didn't overpower him or didn't do something because I wasn't the leader per se. We understood each other, and we were confident with the roles that we each had.

When it came to creativity, my husband knew that I was more creative, so I would plan the events and activities for the group. When it was about putting a plan of action together and writing out processes, he was more effective in doing those. It just worked for us. It wasn't till about eleven years into our marriage when I started working as a full time Entrepreneur and he was full time in corporate America, that I realized that all along we have been doing what so many couples or men and women leadership teams desire to have. Which is understanding, cohesiveness, clarity and the ability to love what we both did. We had so many couples, organizations and families that came to us wondering how we are so effective in what we do. It's simple!

"If you are not living your life on purpose, you are simply alive and not living"

Tweet

Dr. Carolyn

We knew our purpose, we understood our strengths and weaknesses which made us aware of what resources we needed to get or hire to succeed. We worked as a team. We cleared the bases. We knew and worked our goals, understood our vision and values. We were like minded in our belief system and we didn't attempt to be something that we were not. That didn't work for us.

From the hurts, frustrations and knowing what worked and what didn't work on a personal level, made us even more effective leaders professionally, because home was where we learned to lead first. These learned behaviors were the blueprint that we used to create coaching templates, consulting services and masterclasses that for team leadership. They are used in organizations, homes, churches and enterprises for those looking for team leadership. It outlines how she leads versus how he leads.

When there's an understanding of the differences between male and female leaders, it makes leading exciting. Whether it's brother and sister, husband and wife, he or she executives, father and daughter, mother and son, opposite sex friendship or any male and female combination that work cohesively together towards one common goal, when it is implemented correctly, the duo are unstoppable.

Personal & Professional Team Leadership

Meet Joel & Victoria Osteen

One of the keys to effective Team Leadership is balance. You may have heard the following expression: 'variety is the spice of life.' One of the traits that is usually found in effective leaders is their ability to strike that balance in their lives that ensures a **stable core, making sure that home is taken care of first**. For example, a leader who is married, have children, lead a company or organization, and has a hobby, and exercise their faith, can only effectively do so, if there's a balance. This leader will experience demands from each of these areas of life, and the key is to balance each of those areas and leave none unattended.

As a leader in the example above, let's say home is the core and everything else are balanced around the home. The leader's faith is their guide and individual time is secured for meditation. The leader's marriage is priority and quality time is dedicated for attention, affection, and conversation making the spouse know, believe, feel, and think, that they are the most important person in the world. The leader's kids crave attention and looks to mom or dad for affirmation, guidance, and play-time. The leader's occupation is where their skills and abilities are used to serve other people. The leader's hobby is his or her 'out.' This is doing an activity that frees their mind from the world around them.

Now, what if this leader spends 80% of time on their occupation while the other areas of their life starves. Their spouse is not getting quality time, their kids rarely sees them, no time is made for a hobby and little time is given to exercising his or her faith. This leader is out of **balance** and before long will experience the dreaded effects of a failing marriage, kids who are disconnected, no sense of purpose or belonging (no faith connection) although their career may seem to be prospering. This will eventually lead to unhealthy mental and physical overload. How can this be prevented?

One of my admired leadership team in our nation today is Joel & Victoria Osteen. Born Joel Scott Osteen, March 5, 1963, in Houston, Texas; Joel is the son of John (a minister) and Dodie Osteen. Joel married Victoria Iloff in 1987 and they have two blessed children: Jonathan and Alexandra. Joel is one of six children in their own family unit. He attended Oral Roberts University in Oklahoma, the largest Christian charismatic university in the world, but returned home after a year and suggested to his parents that he set up a television ministry for Lakewood Church.

From No to Yes – decisions require re-balancing

For the next 15 years Osteen directed and produced the weekly Sunday service at Lakewood, which aired on a local Houston station, and later on the Family Channel, a cable network. He traveled with his father, even as far as India, to assist in the church's missionary and outreach work. Occasionally, his father asked if he would like to deliver a sermon or speak during the church services—but he declined the invitation. By early 1999, John Osteen's health was deteriorating, and he felt increasingly taxed by heart and kidney problems one week. He asked his son to deliver the Sunday sermon, and Osteen once again refused—but then called back a few minutes later and told his father that he would do it. Nervous and wearing a pair of his father's shoes for emotional support, Osteen spoke that day before a crowd of 6,000, and the churchgoers responded well to his easygoing, affable style. Eleven days later, his father died of a heart attack, and Osteen was named successor of the ministry.

Under Joel's leadership, Lakewood church has grown to more than 30,000 members. His televised sermons are seen by over 7 million viewers weekly and over 20 million monthly in over 100 countries. Osteen's Sunday sermons were broadcast weekly on religious channels such as TBN and showed up on cable channels that included ABC Family, USA, and BET. Osteen also had his own show, *Joel Osteen,* and have toured U.S. cities in one-night speaking engagements called "Night of Hope" that drew thousands to arenas.

Home First

From the outside looking in, it is not difficult to see that Joel has establish himself as an effective leader at home first. His decision to lead Lakewood demanded that he re-evaluated his personal life and responsibilities to sustain good balance. Let's look at some telltale signs of Joel establishing balance in his life.

1. Faith & Ministry – At Lakewood, much of his work week is spent writing and practicing his Sunday sermon, and spending time with the Lord, while other Lakewood ministers handle the bulk of the other pastoral duties—weddings, funerals, and other engagements.

2. Marriage, Kids, and hobby – Joel's view on prosperity is an indication he is not one dimensional but has what our Firm calls "whole life" mindset. In an interview with the *Texas Monthly* article, Joel stated, "Prosperity is not just money, **It's a healthy relationship with your wife, with your kids; it's a healthy body**. We need to get away from the dollar sign on prosperity." Osteen is nearly always seen with his wife, Victoria, by his side. Their two young children, Alexandra and Jonathan, also take an active role in Sunday services. Joel in his sermons has on occasion

shared stories about his time in the gym, which would be his "out."

Joel's own success is mirrored in the success of his wife Victoria who Co-Pastor's with her husband. As a wife and mother of two, Victoria is an inspiration and example to women everywhere who are balancing responsibilities both inside and outside the home. She is committed to empowering women, children, and families to connect and grow strong with a foundation of faith in Jesus Christ. This commitment and passion led her to begin the women's ministry at Lakewood Church which equips women at every age and every stage in life—at home, in relationships, and in the workplace. Every week, Victoria hosts a live, call-in radio show on Joel Osteen Radio positively influencing the lives of many listeners around the world

Sources: https://www.joelosteen.com/Pages/AboutVictoria.aspx.

http://www.notablebiographies.com/newsmakers2/2006-Le-Ra/Osteen-Joel.html#ixzz5DKHSxaCX

Joel & Victoria's effectiveness in leading together was and is contingent on their abilities to balance home and work. Since they had a strong foundation of leadership at home, it was easier for them to lead together outside of the home. I would imagine that they had a process in place similar to what my husband and I have, that is, to have weekly **staff meetings** at home. Our staff meetings consist of an agenda that includes everything from our marriage to the kids' school schedule. We involve the children in our meetings as well. If they didn't have a system in place at home, it would have been virtually impossible to oversee such a MEGA organization. In addition, they don't do it alone. It requires a strong team that understands and knows the vision and values of the church. Joel and Victoria do not just oversee Lakewood Church, but they have books, television ministry and other businesses that they run together. Team Leadership is organizational leadership whether inside or outside the home.

Organizational Leadership

Leadership as defined by Lussier & Achua (2013) states that "Leadership *is the influencing process of leaders and followers to achieve organizational objectives through change*" (p. 5). They went on to say that leadership has five key elements, namely: Influence, Organizational Objectives, People, Change, and Leaders-Followers and each key element carries its own set of values. Organizational Leadership can be very tricky. Every organization has its own culture, principles and values, as well as each department within the organization.

When I worked in the Sales Department of an organization and was later promoted to the Contracting Department the cultures were so different, even though it was within the same company. In fact, where I sat when I was in the Sales Department was directly outside the door of where I ended up sitting for the Contracting Department. My office in Contracting and the cubicle in Sales were like a reflection of each other, yet it was like I came from an outside organization and now working somewhere new. What was different? The people were different, thus, there's a variation in beliefs, values, aspirations and mindsets. I had to learn and adapt to the culture of the Contracting Department in order to be a successful team member. This is true for any organization, business and even household – cultures vary.

The culture of an organization is shaped by the people that makes up an organization. According to www.dictionary.com, an organization is "a group of persons' organized for some end or work." An organization does not exist without people. A building is just a shell and serve no purpose empty. It cannot do anything or accomplish any purpose on its own, besides housing the people that will work in it. The key to organizational leadership success is to have a culture that is healthy always leaving room for growth.

The traditional organizational structure that still exist in some organizations today, will need to transform, otherwise it will eventually evaporate. Look at what happened to Blockbuster, Blackberry Phones and other former successful businesses that remained the same or was slow to change when the market demanded a change. Today they do not exist. Blackberry might still have some units functioning, but nowhere compared to Apple or Samsung phone products.

"An organization, no matter how well designed, is only as good as the people who live and work in it."

Dee Hock

Leadership is different today from what it was years ago and so should the organizational structures. The typical structure is not effective anymore and if organization's wanting to keep up with the trend and the direction that success is heading, then companies need to move away from traditional to strategic. Below is an example of a typical organizational structure. There's normally boxes or rectangles with a hangman look and often times, the organizational charts only show the leadership team or those who are considered the top leaders. Not everyone within the organization makes the list.

Traditional Organizational Chart Example:

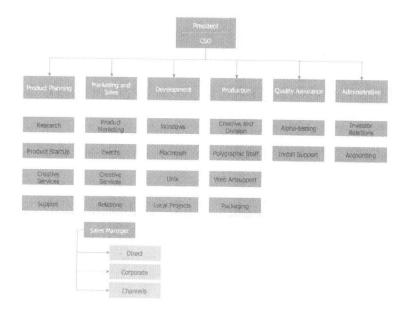

Image copied from Google Search

http://www.conceptdraw.com/How-To-Guide/organization-structure

The leadership structures that has proven to work well within the organizations that I lead and those that our Firm has helped, is shaped like a human being (a body). At the top of the organizational chart is a head. Meaning the image is shaped literally like a physical head. The neck is the CEO or second in command, the shoulders are the Executive Team, then the hands, legs, fingers toes, etc., all team members of the body. Having a body-shaped organizational chart, shows and tells everyone in the organization where they belong and how valuable they are. It shows that all parts of the body (the entire team) are necessary and essential and no one position is greater than the other. The hand needs the arm and the fingers to operate, and a head is just a head, if it has no body.

This concept has worked so well for us. Our Consulting Firm has been recognized for its ingenuity, leadership, creativity, strategy and being different. Everyone feels and sees where they belong in the organization and how valuable they are. It also includes other roles that the organization needs to succeed, similar to how the body needs food to survive. Integrity Consulting Enterprise need its affiliates, publicist, attorneys etc., to survive and our organizational chart shows that as well. I believe that's the paradigm shift that a lot of organizations are moving towards or have moved towards. It's just not reflected in their structure. Employees are more productive, when they are able to see where they fit into the overall organization which eventually generates more profits.

I would suggest that organizations whose philosophy is that their employees are their #1 customer, should employ this structure. This is the new norm for organizational leadership. The old paradigm of leadership has expired. Gone are the days where organizations are what's considered top heavy, with more senior management and 'bosses' than direct reports. There are so many employees who dislike the work that they do. To them, it's just a job that's paying the bills and that's it. A new day has arrived. It's a new dawning. New leadership is here. It's time for a change.

Do you see yourself as valuable in your organization? Explain

NOTES..........

Journal the Journey – Notes from this Chapter

CHAPTER 9

LAW #9: THE SHIPS

LEAD-ER-SHIP, CORPORATE-SHIP, ENTREPRENEUR-SHIP, FOLLOWER-SHIP, RELATION-SHIP, FRIEND-SHIP

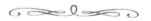

"Leadership is practiced not so much in words as in attitude and in actions."

Harold S. Geneen

Leadership is a difficult concept to define, because leadership is personal. No two human beings are alike, which means that there are no two like traits, vision, purpose and DNA that are alike. Not even identical twins, in the same womb, have the same identical

DNA. Since leadership is personal and leadership is about purpose, it's difficult to define. A leader who doesn't know his or her purpose, is not a leader at all. That person is a follower.

Secondly different generations lead differently, which affects leadership styles. Then there are cultural, gender and economic differences which affects leadership styles as well. How can one wrap leadership up into one definition? You really can't because leadership is so broad. With all those aspects and more, there still remains fundamental principles that are pillars for leadership. It is no different from the laws of our land and the 10 Commandments given in the bible - they exist – and so does the 10 Laws of Leadership.

The Leadership principles are being re-established, they are real and for those who truly want to lead, it's imperative that he or she is guided by the laws of leadership. Purpose must be established, skills and traits must be displayed and respecting how he leads versus how she leads, will keep the SHIP on its right path. In this time and era, mankind cannot afford for the SHIP to be lost again and end up in the middle of nowhere, stranded with no means of getting back on shore. The Legacy of the Generations that will be the leaders that carries on the torch is contingent on re-building the laws of leadership. Your children and children's children need leadership to be positioned on the right path so that they will know how to lead authentically and live purposefully amidst chaos. For this is what leadership is all about.

An authentic (reliable, dependable, faithful, and trustworthy) leader is a leader who has visions, sound values, grounded in their beliefs, and care about the people they lead. An effective leader can be trusted to create a passage plan, reliable in ensuring all his or her crew knows the plan, dependable in executing the plan, trustworthy and honest about the state of the plan, and faithful in executing the plan daily to the best of their ability.

THE -ER-

Leaders must always be prepared to lead on the calm waters as well as on the rough seas. It is what our organization like to call the "**Lead-ER's**" for leaders: **ER's are Emergency Response** situations. A good leader not only considers the best-case scenarios. They must also consider the worst-case scenarios in every situation. After creating the passage plan, a leader must also perform situational analysis or what-if scenarios. These types of analysis can be applied to individual factors, internal factors, external factors and unforeseen factors. Conducting these types of analysis and implementing countermeasure plans, sets a leader up for success in **ER** situations.

Take for example airlines such as American Airline, Southwest, and Delta; their pilots go through simulation training. During the simulation training, the pilots are presented with many emergency type scenarios such as engine failure, stuck landing gear, faulty instrumentation, etc. The pilots must then make decisions how to navigate the aircraft during these failure modes and successfully land the plane. The simulation training, one could hypothesize, are key factors in pilots being able to successfully navigate flights to a safe landing. Any deviation from following through on specific instructions in these emergency situations could lead to catastrophic failures. Therefore, it is in the best interest of leaders to conduct situation analysis and what-if scenarios to ensure contingency plans are in place to navigate emergency situation as they navigate their ship in the sea of business.

In the examples above you were introduced to the concept of "Lead-ER", and now let's look at another element, which is the S.H.I.P. In the examples above, integrity is one of the leadership attributes that was highlighted as it was applicable to the stories. However, integrity is only one of the attributes that is key to leadership. Leaders who are captains of organizations or their own entrepreneurial ventures must have the S.H.I.P. to successfully develop and execute their passage plan.

"If the highest aim of a captain were to preserve his ship, he would keep it in port forever."

Thomas Aquinas

CORPORATE-SHIP

"Corporate cultures matter. How management chooses to treat its people impacts everything – for better or for worse"

Simon Sinek

When Gordon Bethune took over the job as CEO of Continental Airlines in 1994, he inherited a mess. According to Entrepreneur Magazine, The Leadership Issue, March 2014, when Bethune took over, the company was losing $55 million per month and was heading to declare bankruptcy for the third time in 10 years. Note, the article didn't say $55 million a year, which would equate to about 1.1 million a month. Nope, it was losing $55 million per month. Continental Airlines was ranked last among the top 10 airlines, in service, customer complaints and baggage handling. Was it even possible to turn things around?

The expenses were added up by the day and things were not looking good for Bethune. He decided to activate his leadership skills to see if he could possible turn things around. What he quickly realized was that the company had not invested in their #1 asset, their employees. Any great leaders know that those on your team are the number one assets, because employees can make a company or break it. What Bethune did have been noted as one of the greatest turnarounds in history for an organization. He unlocked the value and potential in Continental's 45,000 employees, because he knew that poor operations are a direct result of poor employee morale.

He implemented a plan of action that rewarded the employees financially on a monthly basis, for every time that Continental was ranked at least in the top five of the 10 airlines companies measured by the Department of Transportation. By 1995, Continental Airlines ranked first in on time performance among major airlines. It started being profitable again and had record income earnings for 11 straight quarters, upping its share price from $3.25 to $50. Bethune retired in 2004, but his style and substance have made him a legend in the airline industry. He's also known as the poster boy for the notion that good leadership has a demonstrable effect on a company's bottom line. Indeed, that is an accurate statement.

When real leaders show up, anything is possible. This is why the pillars of leadership needs to be re-built, because one leader can transform a dying organization into a thriving one. All it takes is a strategy, motivated followers that trust you, drive and endurance. Continental Airlines could have continued its path to bankruptcy and potential closure. Its legacy could have been tainted with the fact that it failed. The Airline later merged with United Airlines and became one organization. That would not have been possible if Bethune would not have turned the company around. There's an organization, family or community that's waiting your leadership to turn it around. You too can turn death into life.

There are several other leaders out there that are making a difference in people's lives. Some are known and some unknown. There's also a new set of leaders who now holds the baton and are ready to run his or her race. Learning from leaders who have led with Integrity and Grit through tough times serves as a key that can be used to unlock all the success that awaits you. Lead well!

 "A ship in port is safe, but that's not what ships are built for."

Grace Hopper

On every **SHIP** there are some standard instruments or components that are critical to that ship's voyage from start to finish. These includes but is not limited to the following: Gyro Compass – used for finding the right direction; Radar – used to determine the distance of the ship from land, other ships, or any floating objects out at sea; Echo Sounder – used to measure depth of the water below the ship's bottom using sound waves; Rudder – helps with turning the ship; GPS - display system used to show the ship's location with the help of Global positioning satellite in the earth's orbit; Voyage Plan - a procedure to develop a complete description of a vessel's voyage from start to finish.; Daylight signaling lamp – used for emergency signaling in the day time.

Source: https://www.marineinsight.com/marine-navigation/30-types-of-navigational-equipment-and-resources-used-onboard-modern-ships/

Like the standard equipment and components in ships. Leader-ship is also associated with some standard equipment. Using the S.H.I.P. in lead-er-<u>ship</u> as an acronym, let's highlight some of the key elements of leadership:

S – Strategy & Sustainable

Every leader must have a strategy to execute their vision. The strategy must be sustainable to endure changing business climates. The strategy is key to a leader delivering business results and assessing performance. Without a strategy, a business or individual may be at risk of achieving their goals.

H – Humility & Honest

Every leader must lead with humility and honesty. Arrogance in leadership limits creativity and creates a culture that lacks innovation. Humility opens a leader to embrace new ideas and creative solutions and approaches. Honesty creates an environment of openness, which allows performance wins and losses to be communicated and addressed appropriately. information is tied to communication. to be shared promptly with corresponding action.

I – Integrity, Information, Implementation

Integrity is the responsibility to be truthful and trustworthy to self and your team. It is holding true to your values and beliefs regardless of the consequence. It is conveying the truth of a matter to evoke urgent responses with the chaos. Leaders must be able to provide timely and frequent status to their teams relative to the overall passage plans. Implementation is directly tied to execution. Poor execution could lead to batch implementation, which could impact the bottom line. In essence, a leader needs a vision, a sustainable strategy, lead with honesty, humility, and integrity and good communication and execution to ensure successful implementations.

P – Purpose, People, & Process

Every leader must know their purpose. Purpose is knowing your reason for existence. It's using your gifts, talents and ability to serve others. People are the most important assets. Leadership does not exist without people. People hold the knowledge and ability for leaders to realize their vision. People create processes, manage processes, design and create products and find solutions to problems, etc. Process is the vehicle used to execute strategies. Processes are like bowling lanes that help a leader to determine how well they are executing. Without good processes it can be difficult for leaders to assess effectiveness of their performance.

As noted through-out this entire book, there are certain characteristics that Leaders must have. One of them is the ability to be able to execute and to be a trendsetter. Leaders must be able to start something, like giving birth. One of the latest phenomenon that's taking over is Entrepreneurship. There are so many conferences, books, teachings and the likes, about Entrepreneurship. However, one of the myths or mis-conceptions that has been taught about Entrepreneurship is that it's a solo job. It is not a one man or woman show and to be an effective Entrepreneur, you need a team and must actually have a product or service that pays. What many are calling Entrepreneurship today are actually hobbies. It's not set up like a real business. There's no phone number to call to get questions answered, and everything is done via email, probably with some gal or lad, in his or her pajamas working from home. While this may be cute to start, that is not true Entrepreneurship. If there's no office to meet, no assistant to call or no team to assist you, that's NOT Entrepreneurship, or I should say, full time Entrepreneurship.

There are many who are Entrepreneurs, but also have one, two or multiple other jobs that they use as a source of income. Yes, building a business from the ground is a lot of work, and I wouldn't recommend Entrepreneurship to just anyone, because it takes a lot of strength, tenacity, tears, and drive to be an Entrepreneur. It is by far one of the most difficult things I have done. All is well when you go to work, and you know for sure that you're going to get paid in a couple weeks. However, when you're an Entrepreneur, you have to hustle to get paid and most times it's not on a consistent basis. Also, something folks will want the Entrepreneur to do the work for free. It's time to shift the mind and create a new paradigm of what Entrepreneurship is all about. It is building a business, having profits, thriving and leaving a legacy for others to follow.

ENTREPRENEUR-SHIP

Meet Valerie Daniels-Carter & John Daniels

"Life is like the monkey bars: you have to let go to move forward. Once you make the decision to leap into entrepreneurship, be sure to loosen your grasp on old concepts so you can swing your way to new ones."

Leah Busque

Mrs. Valerie Daniels-Carter, along with her brother John started V & J Foods with a single Burger King restaurant in 1982. Within sixteen years, she nurtured the company into a 137-unit, multi-brand operation. First and foremost, Mrs. Daniels-Carter is a God-fearing woman. Her key beliefs include an insistence on: integrity, recognition, accountability, responsibility, respect, communication, commitment to excellence and passion. Mrs. Daniels- Carter has a hands-on approach. She focuses on the performance of each and every unit so that all are achieving positive results. Her corporate philosophy is "YATSE": You are the Standard of Excellence. Mrs. Daniels-Carter laid the foundation for her successful career at Lincoln University where she received her

Bachelor of Science degree in Business Administration. She later earned a Master of Science degree in Management from Cardinal Stritch University. Valerie Daniels-Carter is one of the best known fast-food operators in the United States.

In addition to owning and running successfully brands for two of the largest fast-food operations in the United States, she has teamed up with one of NBA's most famous and valuable players, Shaquille O'Neal, to expand the horizons of Auntie Anne's famous Pretzels. VJ & O'Neal Enterprises, LLC was established in 2006 by V&J and O'Neal Franchise. VJ & O' Neal rolled out its first Auntie Anne's soft Pretzel Corporation into the Eastland Mall in Harper Wood, MI with plans for several more.

Valerie Daniels-Carter has been widely recognized for her business judgment, having served on financial and corporate boards, and have led civic and business organizations. She is recognized by Essence Magazine as one of the 50 most admired African-Americans in the United States, joining the company of Oprah Winfrey and Colin Powell.

Source: About Valerie Daniels Carter (www.vjfoods.com)

Lessons learned about Entrepreneur-SHIP

Valerie and her brother John have created an empire. They are the epiphany of Entrepreneurship. Valerie started out solo, like most Entrepreneurs do, but she didn't stay that way. She recognized that if she was going to rise to the top, she needed a team, diversity in investments and she needed to show that she means business. Money is influence, because money talks. They have built a legacy that others can learn from, teaching us that all things are possible when you put your mind to it. She is unstoppable, and it will only be more successful for her as she travels the path of true Entrepreneurship. Just like my Firms, it was started with the mindset of doing it alone, but that quickly changed when I realize that true Entrepreneurship is about Leadership and effective Leadership is about actually leading. If I'm a one-woman corporation, then I truly wouldn't be leading, I would just be taking a walk in the park, alone, solo, without a following.

FOLLOWER-SHIP

"A functioning, robust democracy requires a healthy educated, participatory follower-ship, and an educated morally grounded leadership."

Chinua Achebe

Leadership does not exist without followership. For one to be called a leader, he or she must have a following, a team or someone that they are leading. There are followers today who are looking for someone to lead them, as followers are also leaders or leaders in training. Take for example the Vice President of the United States of America. He's a leader from the second seat, and also a follower. He has a set of people that reports to him and he eventually reports to the President.

Followership is the ability to follow and lead at the same time. It's similar to being a servant-leader, where you serve before you lead. As a matter of fact, most leadership positions are really servitude positions, because an effective leader is more concerned about the well-being of those he or she leads, than even their own, and that is servant-leadership.

While I am a leader, I am also a follower. At times when I am in certain positions, I become the follower. There are times when decisions need to be made at home and I step back and allow my husband to take the leadership role in certain situations. When I go to someone else's organization even as a Consultant, I am not the leader of that organization, but rather operating in the followership role or servitude mode.

Followership is a gift and it's a strength when a leader is so confident about his or herself that following is not seen as a threat but as a gift. My nieces and nephews look up to me and they love being around me, yet, my leadership for them is temporal, since they only spend weekends with me or summer holidays. My brother is their leader and probably the one they look up to, even though leadership can be followed from a distance. The morale of the story is that, followership can be a desired role, because some of the greatest Leaders, if not all, started off by being excellent followers. I was one of them. It gives me great joy to be lead, because it shows humility, honor and grace. Followership is one of the fundamental principles that builds great relationships and creates an environment that is conducive for growth.

RELATION-SHIP

"I think for any relationship to be successful, there needs to be loving communication, appreciation, and understanding."

Miranda Kerr

Life exits within four (4) quadrants, namely, your Health, Finance, Relationships and Faith. Pretty much everything in life, falls into one of those categories. I have a book that I wrote called Healthy Life-Healthy-Land that became best seller in less than one hour after it launched. In that book, I share about taking responsibility and ownership of having healthy relationships.

A leader with great relationship skills is like the image of a rainbow in the sky. It comes in different colors and sizes, but when put together in its proper place, it leaves one in awe. On a rainbow, the colors are never out of order. They follow the pattern as created by God. A rainbow is very captivating especially when you can see the entire circle that it forms. I've seen those wonderful circular rainbows around the sun and it takes your breath away.

Rainbows however, do not appear in the sky until after a storm or beyond the reflections of the cloud. So is the sight of a relationship, they become stronger after the storms whether in your personal or professional life. A relationship whether mother and child, spouses, best friends, co-workers, etc., must be tested and only the strong ones will survive.

Every relationship will come to a point where there's a conflict, where there's a choice to be made. It comes to a point where the authenticity and strength of the relationship undergoes a test. Some tests are long, and some are short. This is when you truly get to see others for who they are and when they show who you they are, you should probably believe them. When situations get rough, such as with Starbucks, Facebook, Amazon and others, it takes strong relationships to maintain the foundation of the organization. This is when the fight or flight syndrome kicks in. People will leave you or stay and fight with you.

There are some relationships that are not healthy, they are toxic. This is in the workplace and in homes and this will affect your leadership style if you're in a toxic relationship. It will affect how you lead, because what tends to happen is, leaders can sometimes portray their brokenness and despair onto their followers. This creates a problem. If you find yourself in an unhealthy situation, it's a good thing to take a step back-pause-evaluate-re-calibrate and seek help and advice if needed.

Amidst the many scandals that's happening in our world today as it relates to abuse, the nature of relationships has changed. Co-workers are tentative to do or say anything. Leaders are afraid to even compliment a co-worker especially one of the opposite sex. What was once appropriate to say in the workplace, may be deemed as in-appropriate today. Therefore, a leader should be aware about the different kinds of relationship that he or she has. Know who you can joke with or who you can't. This will protect your leadership in the long run. Create boundaries that works best for you.

FRIEND-SHIP

"One of the most beautiful qualities of true friendship is to understand and to be understood."

Lucius Annaeus Seneca

Like relationships, friendships are also necessary for leaders to have and to be. Some of the best friends that we have today, started off as friendship in the workplace. In fact, many marriages today started off as friendships in the workplace, which probably led to a relationship and then marriage. Depending on the employer, one or both of the spouses had to leave the department or the company in general based on certain company policies.

Leaders need friends that they trust and are able to share experiences with. Since leadership can be such a lonely place, having healthy friendships can prevent isolations for leaders. Friendships are like therapy. Having someone you can run ideas by, or just share a scenario with to get a different perspective on the situation.

Friendships are such powerful forces, that there are friends who have built successful companies together. Facebook started off by two friends and then evolved into solo ownership. There are several other companies, some very successful who are being ran today by best friends. I personally know of a company that is worth about 30 million dollars, who are being ran by two college buddies. They started the company from inception together and today it's worth millions. This is why friendships is one of the SHIPS in the 10 Laws of Leadership. Now is a good time to re-build healthy friendships that are goal oriented, focus minded and have a purpose. Once both parties understand each other and understand the purpose of the friendship, there should not be any conflicts.

**NOTES..........**

Journal the Journey – Notes from this Chapter

NOTES..........

Journal the Journey – Notes from this Chapter

CHAPTER 10

LAW #10: COMMUNICATION - LIFE OR DEATH

 "The art of communication is the language of leadership."

James Humes

In 2003, a 17-year-old female name Jessica, had a surgical transplant for a new heart and lung. She went into surgery excited to wake up with a new heart and lung. I can only imagine how thrilled Jessica must have been considering that she was getting two new organs that she probably desperately needed. I cannot fathom what it's like to need major organs especially at such a young age, and so having both available must have been a dream come through for her. There must have been several tests that were performed prior to Jessica having her surgery, because it was noted that her blood type was O.

Jessica had her surgery and unfortunately her body rejected the organs. The organs she received was from a Donor with a Type A blood type. How could that have been missed? From the laboratory, to the nurses, the doctors, the surgeons, the hospital and all that's involved in surgical procedures, how could that have been missed? Jessica had a second surgery that was from a donor with the right blood type, but unfortunately, she later passed away due to global cerebral hypoxic injury that was a complication of the rejection of an incompatible heart-lung transplant from her first surgery.

Due to the extent of the damage caused after the first surgery, it was too much for her body to handle and she died. Mis-communication cost Jessica her life as well as countless others. This miscommunication still happens today, unfortunately. This is why effective communication is one of the Laws of Leadership. Mis-communication can produce life, or it can be deadly. In the case of Jessica, it was simple as making sure that there was effective communication of Jessica's blood type and the donors. That should have been clearly communicated. It should not have gotten to the point of costing Jessica her life. Had this been communicated effectively, Jessica could have been alive today.

This is why communication can be life or death situations. It can save lives or destroy them. It can excel in business or make it go bankrupt.

Source: https://onlinelibrary.wiley.com/doi/full/10.1111/j.1600-6143.2012.04139.x

Houston, Houston we have a problem! May day, May day! Do You Copy! Roger That! Over! 10-4! – these are variations of languages and codes that are used as methods of communication. Effective Communication is one of the most critical aspects of effective leadership. If you think about it, everything in this book is all about communication. Whether that's communicating our values, beliefs, vision, mission, strengths, weaknesses or applying any principle in this book, it all boils down to communication.

Communication can be the Anchor or the Sail of a Ship. Both elements are necessary components of a Ship, but they are used for different reasons, during different times. The anchor needs to stand still and hold the ship in position when the Ship is docked, or in-between voyages. It would be a disaster to set sail, with the anchor dragging along at the sea-bed and never in its right position, because no one communicated to the team that it was time to set sail.

The same is true for the Sail. When the ship is at sea and ready for its new journey, the sail needs to operate as it should. It's a guide for the ship and it helps to chop against the winds for directional purposes. When the ship is anchored, it's not necessary for the sail to be in position to soar. While both are necessary, both are needed at the same time. So, it is for communication. A leader should employ the proper communication language based on what he or she is attempting to communicate.

A Leader cannot use the same language to communicate to an investor as they do with a supplier. It is two different languages. A Leader cannot share with his competitors the strategy that's in place for growth. How, what, where and why something is being communicated, must be carefully examined so avoid a death situation.

In the example with Jessica while extreme, it happens more often than one things. Mis-communication has caused wrong limbs to be amputated, airplane crashes, wrong administration of a drug, expulsion from school, deadly bacteria in water, car accidents, and mechanical failures. In light of all the technological advancements, such as emails, instant messages, snapchat, texting etc., there's even a greater need for leaders to exercise effective methods of communication. I coach my staff how to over-communicate to ensure that the message is received.

We are one of the very few Coaching firms that has an actual corporate phone number, where you can speak with a real person. Most of the entrepreneurial ventures today are just emails or online chats. Corporations like doing business with us, because of our methods of communication. We will call, email and text our customers, coachees and clients to make sure that there's an open line of communication. Communication is also more than written methods. There are non-verbal gestures and new body languages that leaders should stay abreast of. Sometimes when I see the young people doing their form of sign language, I have to ask one of my daughter's what does that mean.

Things are changing rapidly and therefore having effective methods of communication will help you keep up with time and be ahead of the game. I teach effective communication skills at a technical college and it's one of the best things courses that I teach, because I learn new things as I'm teaching the course. One of the concepts that have helped me, and the business is how to communicate with other global leaders. I've learned what not to say or do if I am meeting with leaders in other countries with cultural differences. Since we are a global organization, we incorporated global strategies. If you are a leader of an organization or starting your own business, I would suggest that you have our Firm come in and do a Communications Training.

This is the 10th Law and perhaps one of the more critical ones. I have seen companies close their doors, downsizing, product failures, terminations, bankruptcies and divorces where the root cause stemmed from a communication mis-understanding. It's very difficult to bounce back from mis-communications. It's achievable, but it takes time and sometimes can damage reputations. People sometimes are not that forgiving. One simple mistake or communication flaw can change the trajectory of your destiny, your legacy, and your life. Therefore, apply effective communication skills in your everyday life, whether personally or professionally. Let it be a habit to have. Let people know you for your effective communication skills, because remember it can be life or death, so choose life.

NOTES..........

Journal the Journey – Notes from this Chapter

SUMMARY

"Leadership is the capacity to translate vision into reality."

Warren Bennis

Every leader needs a vision and every vision needs a strategy. Every strategy needs a plan of execution, and every plan of execution needs a counter measures or contingency plan. Two of the most fascinating transportation inventions I believe are Ships, and Airplanes. Both have experienced tremendous enhancements in their navigation capabilities because of technology and innovation. As advanced as these two equipment's are, airplanes are still required to file flight plans. **A flight plan** describes a proposed aircraft **flight**. It involves two safety-critical aspects: fuel calculation, to ensure that the aircraft can safely reach the destination, and compliance with air traffic control requirements, to minimize the risk of midair collision and other accidents that can happen. (https://en.wikipedia.org/wiki/Flight_planning)

Likewise, ships are also required to create a Passage plan or Passage Planning. **Passage planning, or voyage planning** is a procedure to develop a complete description of a vessel's voyage from start to finish. The plan includes leaving the dock and harbor area, the *en-route* portion of a voyage, approaching the destination, and mooring (permanent structure to which a ship will be secured), the industry term for this is 'berth to berth'. According to international law, a vessel's captain is legally responsible for passage planning.

(https://en.wikipedia.org/wiki/Passage_planning)

Leaders are the captain of their organization (the SHIP). Like the captain of a ship, leaders are legally responsible for business passage planning for the organization they lead. One example of a company in recent history with a captain that violated their responsibility to their passage planning is Enron. What they did was illegal and cost a lot of heartaches, destruction, prison time and loss of life. When leaders fail to create and execute their passage plan with integrity, it usually ends in disaster, as was the case with Enron. Enron was hiding and covering up financial losses and using deceitful means in their accounting practices.

What Enron did is like a captain of a ship who intentionally chose to neglect the passage plan that protects them and their crew and choosing their own self-interest over the interest of the business, stakeholders, and investors. Using manipulative means is not the mark of a true leader. Using deceit is self-inflicting and instead of leading the ship through a storm, this type of leader creates the storm.

Leadership and leading has transformed over the years. From generation to generations, from decade to decades, from century to centuries, the transformation of leadership structures has been evident across all industry, organizations and countries around the world. Leadership in the home is different. The structure of a home used to be that the male works outside of the home and the female works inside the home. This has been a complete paradigm shift and that's no longer the case. Actuality there are homes where the woman makes significantly more than the man and that's fine. Organizational structures as I discussed previously have also changed. Over time many organizational structures were developed as governance and operational mechanisms to improve relationships vertically and horizontally, improve products and services, and maximize profits and return on investments.

It is critical that leaders understand the structure of the organization they lead to effectively and successfully deliver business results. Understanding organizational structures, helps a leader to identify potential gaps and the countermeasures needed to navigate those gaps. It also helps a leader to realize the strengths of the organization. One of the activities that our business conduct with various organizations is a S.W.O.T Analysis. S.W.O.T. stands for Strength, Weaknesses, Opportunities and Threats.

Leaders can set themselves up for success by taking the time to complete a S.W.O.T. analysis, not only within the organization, but for various functions, departments, teams, etc. within the organization and personally. A S.W.O.T. analysis is just one of the tools that a leader can use to keep the ship on the water and sailing in the right direction. Transformational leaders not only perform S.W.O.T. analysis on the organization, but also on themselves. The personal S.W.O.T. helps leaders identify gaps within their competencies. Knowing these gaps allows a leader to seek the appropriate resources to aide in their decision making. For example, a non-financial manager may identify a gap in preparing financial analysis and seek help from a financial manager. Knowing these gaps and seeking the right resources to close them could make the difference in the SHIP (the organization) remaining on the right path.

Leadership is about leading authentically, living purposefully, amidst chaos. Society today is in a frenzy and things are continuing to get out of control, however, I believe that you and I can shift leadership back into its position. I believe that the time to establish the 10 Laws of Leadership, is now! No more delay. Let's lead together and live life fully every day.

NOTES..........

Journal the Journey – Notes from this section

CONCLUSION

"The task of the leader is to get his people from where they are to where they have not been."

Henry Kissinger

It's more than a title, it's more than a show, it's more than a name, it's more than a position, it's more than sitting in an office, it's more than being called the CEO, the founder, the owner, the VP, leadership is more than being called boss, or captain, it's more than being the president, the king or the queen. Leadership expands beyond gender, race, color, age, creed, class, or culture. It stretches beyond the horizon of the deep sea, leaps over the boundaries of nations, goes deeper than the ocean floor, it is taller than the highest peak. It cannot be placed in a box or displayed on a shelf.

Leadership doesn't seek fame or notoriety or looks to be praised. Leadership doesn't gravitate for attention or pouts when not noticed. Leadership doesn't see danger and look the other way. Leadership doesn't ignore justice or what's right. It isn't vulgar, disrespectful, vain, or conceited. Leadership doesn't exalt itself or promotes biases. Leadership doesn't desire strife or discontent. It doesn't run into a closet and hide hoping no one will notice that you're not there. Leadership isn't afraid to take risk or even to fail, because failure is an option. Leadership isn't entangled in gossip and hearsay's but seeks truth and solves problems. Leadership doesn't seek out trouble or is arrogant leaving no room for feedback or constructive criticism. Leadership isn't racist, shouldn't discriminate, isn't hateful or wicked. It isn't immoral, selfish, or does not obey the law or is illegal.

Leadership is about living purposefully, leading authentically, having balance, amidst chaos, being able to focus to get results. Leadership is about love, perseverance, tenacity, drive, whit, transparency, vulnerability, teamwork and transformation. and effective use of time. Leadership is being able to distinguish between right or wrong, good and bad. Leadership is about desiring to see others grow, flourish and coaching followers how to be the best person. Leadership is about taking responsibility, being human and ownership. Leadership is about being effective, solving problems, while living life fully every day and using time effectively.

Balance

Whew! How do I do all this, you might be asking? What a book! This is a lot, right? No, it's not! You probably have a slight headache, maybe feeling overwhelmed, like, how am I going to be able to pull all this together. How will I learn how to lead authentically, being myself, yet knowing that I may never be recognized for it? How do I balance my life and lead it well? You're probably pondering, how do I fit all this into my schedule, and manage my time? How do I **do** all this? By balancing your time!

The basic umbrella was invented more than 4,000 years ago. There is evidence of umbrellas in the ancient art and artifacts of Egypt, Assyria, Greece and China. These ancient umbrellas or parasols were first designed to provide shade from the sun. The Chinese were the first to waterproof their umbrellas for use as rain protection. They waxed and lacquered their paper parasols in order to use them for rain.

The word "umbrella" comes from the Latin root word "umbra," meaning shade or shadow. Starting in the 16th century the umbrella became popular in the western world, especially in the rainy climates of northern Europe. At first, it was considered only an accessory suitable for women. Then the Persian traveler and writer Jonas Hanway (1712-86) carried and used an umbrella publicly in England for 30 years. He popularized umbrella use among men. English gentleman often referred to their umbrellas as a "Hanway." In 1852, Samuel Fox invented the steel ribbed umbrella design. Fox also founded the "English Steels Company" and claimed to have invented the steel ribbed umbrella as a way of using up stocks of farthingale stays, the steel stays used in women's corsets.

After that, compact collapsible umbrellas were the next major technical innovation in umbrella manufacture, which arrived over a century later. Now consider the function of the umbrella. The key to it working effectively is keeping all the eight ribs in balance when the umbrella is expanded to the open position. How many of you have seen or had an umbrella where one or more of the ribs were broken? How well did that umbrella function? It looks hideous, the cover sags, and it does not effectively perform its intended purpose.

The umbrella is out of balance. This is what happens when a leader is out of balance. One of the rib in the umbrella is broken. Striking the right balance takes thought, planning and lots of communication. Our company have worked with and provided tools to many leaders, couples, and individual and businesses to help them improve the effectiveness of how to balance their time and not manage it.

Source: https://www.thoughtco.com/who-invented-the-umbrella-1992592.

Time Management or Not?

For starters, **<u>time cannot be managed</u>**, there's no such thing. Time cannot be managed whether in business, personal or professional life. It doesn't exist. There's no such thing as time management and yes, I know, for years, companies have been training, hiring consultants to train about time management, yet there's no such thing. The sun rises when it wants to and sets when it's supposed to.

Time does not stop, hold or stand still for anyone (well, except for Joshua in the bible when he commanded the sun and the moon to stand still, which was God-ordained). Time continues and is constant and cease not. God is the author, finisher, controller of time and only He manages it. It's up to each individual to use the 24 hours that is given in each day effectively. No one has more or less than 24 hours, so use it wisely.

Using time effectively is very doable. Once you learn how to use it effectively, it's a lifesaver. It has saved my life and countless others that have used the product or attended one of my events, a Client or Coachee. It's one of my secrets that I have used for years and now you can too, it's called **Time Mapping™**. People ask me all the time, pretty much every day, how do you do it? In fact, after speaking to me for about fifteen minutes, he or she will say "so tell me what do you not do?" "Do you sleep?" and my answer is always the same. I sleep very well, I don't jump out of airplanes, I work only 24 hours per week and I apply **Time Mapping**™ in my life. It's a principle from a product that I sell called **Time Map**™.

Time Mapping™

Life is a journey and so everything that I teach, that I do and most of my trademarks and products have something to do with a Map, such as Strategic Vision Map™, Purpose Mapping™, etc. (see www.carolynganderson.com). We are on a journey and therefore a map is one of the tools that can be used to get us from one destination to another. It can be used to get a business, career, relationship, finances, leadership, from one level, one season, one dimension to another. If there isn't a map that's being used as a blueprint or guide, then to me, it's like being guided by someone who is not able to see where he or she is going. It's time to start mapping out your time by using the Wheel of Time™ Assessment below.

Time Map™

The Wheel of Time Assessment attempts to show a pictorial view of what you are using your time to do each day. When one can physically see what he or she is using their time to do, it gives a better understanding of time. It also helps you to see if you're wasting time in any are of your life. Being able to plot your time on paper allows you to be more FOCUSED on things that really matter and helps you to become a better leader. Follow the instructions below to get an overview of the balance that currently exists between each of the key areas in your life in order to begin to make the changes necessary to use time effectively. If you are a leader, then it's time to re-evaluate your life, business or career.

After all this, if I were to define leadership, I would say Leadership is living purposefully, showing vulnerability, practicing generosity, displaying authenticity and standing for something - which is called principle. That's a little wordy though, so to sum it all up, Leadership is leading authentically, living purposefully, amidst chaos and using TIME effectively.

Finally, here's a blank circle that represents 24 hours. So, for purposes of this exercise, let's focus on a typical work week, which for most people are 5 days per week. So, reflecting on the past week, what do you spend your time on each day. Using pie shaped pieces that represents time, show on the circle how much time was spent doing what. For example, eight hours should be sleep, and perhaps 8 hours is rest, so what did you use the other 8 hours to do, within a 24-hour period.

Use as an example for mapping out your time

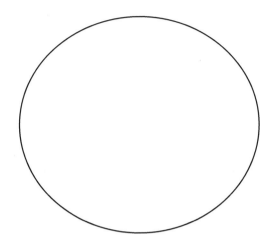

You can use the following image as well to map out your Time

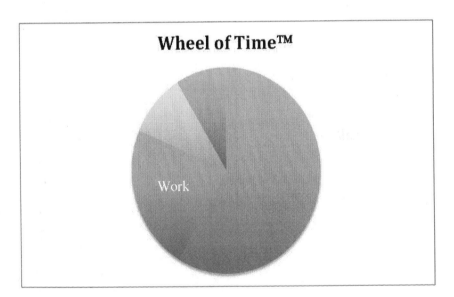

There are several areas of life that each human being has. For the most part most of our lives falls within the following categories below. Take a moment and read through the areas of life and answer the following questions.

The key areas considered include:

1. Career/Business (how much time do you spend working a job, career, occupation)

2. Finances and Wealth (managing your money)

3. Friends and Family (important plutonic, interpersonal, relationships)

4. Fun, Recreation and Entertainment (guiltless, earned pleasure, just stuff)

5. Health and Fitness (exercise, nutrition, workout)

6. Love Life (significant other)

7. Personal/Spiritual Development (meditation, prayer, this is your me time)

8. Physical Environment (your physical space – house, city, state, country)

Questions

1. Rank your level of satisfaction within each area of your life by drawing a single point in each of the 8 segments of the circle displayed on the next page. When plotting your point consider that the center of the wheel = POOR and the outer edge = EXCELLENT.

2. Once you have ranked each segment, draw a line connecting each of the points. The new perimeter represents your Wheel of Time.

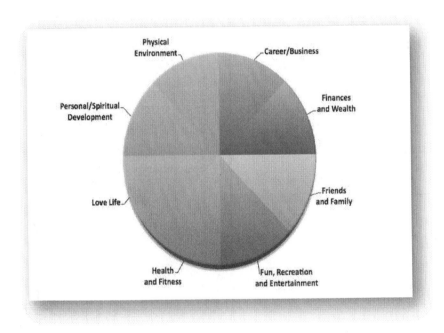

Image from LiFE on Purpose Coaching Module

(www.carolyngandeson.com)

Originally adopted from Benay Wettle

Describe what kind of ride life would be if this was a real wheel based on the points you plotted. Is your life in poor condition, excellent or could use some improvement?

List any life areas that you think you need to work on.

_____

_____

_____

_____

_____

_____

_____

_____

_____

_____

What would you need to do to improve each area of your life?

Career/Business (how much time do you spend working a job, career, occupation)

_____

_____

_____

_____

Finances and Wealth (managing your money)

_____

_____

_____

_____

_____

Friends and Family (important plutonic, interpersonal, relationships)

_____

_____

_____

_____

Fun, Recreation and Entertainment (guiltless, earned pleasure, just stuff)

_____

_____

_____

_____

_____

Health and Fitness (exercise, nutrition, workout)

_____

_____

_____

_____

_____

Love Life (significant other)

_____

_____

_____

_____

_____

Personal/Spiritual Development (meditation, prayer, this is your me time)

_____

_____

_____

_____

_____

Physical Environment (your physical space – house, city, state, count

You did it! The journey is almost over. We are getting ready to bring the ship and shore so that you can explore the land. It's time to put in action that which you have learned while at sea. You are ready to take the necessary steps in life to becoming the great leader that you are. At this juncture as you're getting ready to debark the ship, you should have a vision and mission statement. Your values and beliefs should be solid and clear. You have a plan of action for your goals and you've established a 24 minute per day dream time. You've taken time to do a SWOT analysis and you're aware of the opportunities that awaits you.

You know your purpose, you're confident in your abilities and you have all the tools that you need to be an effective and authentic leader. You are ready to lead authentically, live purposefully, amidst chaos, knowing that you can achieve anything if you just believe. You are ready to activate "**The 10 Laws of Leadership**."

NOTES..........

Journal the Journey – Notes from this section

NOTES..........

Journal the Journey – Notes from this section

EPILOGUE

"Example is leadership."

Albert Schweitzer

I am excited about your new journey and I can't wait to meet you in person at one of my book tours or the Dr. Carolyn Show. If I would have started out this book, by telling you that before going forward that you needed to detox your life, you would have been turned off and probably not read the book. If I would have even mentioned the word detox, you probably would have just shut me out. It would have been an immediate turn-off, trust me, I know. So, I know you've finished reading this book, either through the book club (DrCarolynBookClub on Facebook), or you read it on your own, or perhaps through an employer or university assignment and you're ready to conquer the world and be the best leader that you are and that's phenomenal. I celebrate with you. Great leaders lead by example. Great leaders don't just tell people what to do, but they show them what to do. Great leaders are those who will get their lives in order, before attempting to lead others.

In an effort to Coach you along your leadership journey, it's imperative that you unlearn some of the habits, thoughts and ideas you had before reading this book. You might have thought that reading this book has helped you get rid of some of what you have been taught, that may have limited your belief system, because going through the exercises in this book. That may be the case. However, it's essential that you go through a detoxing process, to get rid of anything that you may or may not know that can hinder your leadership now or in the near future.

When I started my Coaching Firm and went through the modules about letting go, I didn't realize that sub-consciously I was making some decisions based on past events that had occurred in my life. To me, I was over it, but sub-consciously it still existed. The process of detoxing my mind, soul and spirit, helped me to truly let go and to be the leader that I am today.

Sometimes adults don't like going through these exercises, as they may seem redundant or repetitive, but they do work. Ask Tony Robbins. If you've even been to one of Tony's seminar's, he goes through a series of detoxing and letting go. As a matter of fact, her spends an entire day (long day) helping the audience to detox. He even takes it to the extreme of doing a fire walk as an outward sign that you're changed internally. Well this exercise doesn't include a physical fire-walk, but it may feel like you're burning up, when you reflect on some of the exercises. It's only a 21-day exercise and guess what, it's online. This book would have been almost 400 pages, if I were to write out all the contents of the 21-day detox your life module. I could, but I'm sure you've read enough.

Lastly, I suggest that after you've done the 21-day Detox Your Life Exercises, that you re-read this book, preferably as part of our book club, your own book club or with a friend of colleague. Sharing ideas and concepts and doing life with someone is the best way to be successful at leading your ship. You can't do life alone on no-man's island.

To get access to the module at no cost to you, please email our assistant at admin@carolynganderson.com and she will give you the access code so that you don't pay for the Module. I hope to see you online soon. Congratulations on becoming the best you! I believe in you!

NOTES..........

21 DAY Journey

 **NOTES..........**

Journal the Journey – Notes from this section

APPRECIATION

"Give thanks in all circumstances…"

1 Thessalonians 5:18, NIV

What a project! What a journey! This is by far was one of the most difficult, time consuming, thought provoking books that I have written, and it took me quite a bit of time, not because writing is difficult for me, but because I had to narrow it down because there's so much that I could have written about leadership. Life also happened a bit, while writing this book.

I could not have done it by myself, because true leadership is about teamwork. With that being said, there are many who I would like to thank for being a part of this journey with me. First, thank you for reading this book and for desiring to expand your leadership. Thanks to God for giving me wisdom, strength and grace every day. He's super awesome! Thanks to my brilliant, patient, handsome, kind, loving husband, who was there when I had to seclude myself from the noise and he ran our business and household when I couldn't - thanks Kevel A. Anderson, Sr., for your love. Thanks to my three loving (when will you be done, Mom) children, Christina Gabriel, Chassidy Gabriel and AJ. You are one of the reasons why I write this book. You are the Centennials that will lead now and forever. To my Mom Sharon, sisters, brothers, friends, colleagues and acquaintances, thank you. To my Staff Jessica, Michelle, Camila, and the impeccable team at RileyPress.com, thank you. To my Sorority sister and cousin, Sheila Parrish-Spence, thank you for your help. Thanks to my buddy, Patrick Snow, for writing the foreword and for simply being a breath of fresh air, you rock! I am delighted that this book is finally here, and you have all helped me to be the best seller that I am today. Thank you!

Dr. Carolyn

NOTES..........

ABOUT THE AUTHOR

"When your VALUES are clear to you, making decisions becomes easier."

Roy E. Disney

Dr. Carolyn G. Anderson, is the **FRESH**, dynamic and influential VOICE that's creating a buzz locally, nationally and internationally. She's a Talk Show Host, Keynote Speaker, Wealth Coach, Philanthropist and #1International Best Selling Author of several books such as **Living a Wealthy LiFE™ on Purpose**, Focus & Get Results, The MEGA Year, Healthy Life, **Pregnant with a Promise**, What Happens When the Dream Dies? From the **PIT** to the **PALACE** and much more. She's a mom, wife, pastor and friend and enjoys traveling and helping to see others live their lives fully every day. She is the founder of Integrity Consulting & Coaching Firm, a corporate company with its headquarters downtown Chicago at the Hancock Building. They specialize in leadership training, strategic mapping, coaching and values training amongst others. Learn more at www.integritycce.com.

Learn more about Dr. Carolyn at:

www.carolynganderson.com

CONNECT WITH US!

Email:
admin@carolynganderson.com

Facebook:
www.facebook.com/IamDrCarolyn2

Instagram:
www.instagram.com/IamDrCarolyn

Twitter:
www.twitter.com/IamDrCarolyn

Websites:
www.DrCarolynShow.com

www.CarolynGAnderson.com

Facebook Book Club:
#DrCarolynBookClub

OTHER BOOKS BY DR. CAROLYN

PREGNANT WITH A PROMISE

FOCUS & GET RESULTS

Heal-thy LiFE
Heal-thy Land

The MVP Year 2017

New in 2018

Heal-thy LiFE/Heal-thy Land 2nd Edition

Living a Wealthy LiFE on Purpose

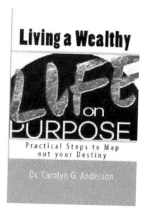

WHAT HAPPENS WHEN THE DREAM DIES?

The MEGA Year 2018

References

Ball, R. (2018, April 20). What's the Role of a Transitional Leader. Retrieved from Personnel Today: https://www.personneltoday.com/hr/whats-the-role-of-a-transitional-leader/

Everything You Need to Know About Transactional Leadership. (2018, April 19). Retrieved from Mindvalley: https://blog.mindvalley.com/transactional-leadership/

Frankl, V. (2006). Man's Search for Meaning. Kindle Edition.

Lussier, R., & Achua, C. (2013). Leadership, theory, application, & skill development. (5th ed.). Mason, OH: South-Western

Munroe, M. (1992). In Pursuit of Purpose. (Destiny Image. Kindle Edition

Shead, M. (2018, April 19). The Functional Leadership Model. Retrieved from Leadership501: http://www.perspectiveonathletics.com/developing-the-3-habits-of-transformational-leaders/

Situational Leadership. (2018, April 17). Retrieved from The Center for Leadership Studies - The Global Home of Situational Leadership: http://situational.com/the-cls-difference/situational-leadership-what-we-do/

Vernonlex, A. (2015, August 27). Developing the Three Habits of Transformational Leaders. Retrieved from Perspective on Athletics: http://www.perspectiveonathletics.com/developing-the-3-habits-of-transformational-leaders/

97407678R00183

Made in the USA
Columbia, SC
11 June 2018